THE MYTH OF THE MARKET

JEREMY SEABROOK was born in Northampton in 1939. He was educated at Northampton Grammar School, at Cambridge University (Gonville & Caius College) and at the L.S.E. In his time he has been a teacher, lecturer and social worker, but in recent years he has become well known as a writer and journalist, contributing regularly to *New Society*, *The Guardian*, and more recently *The Independent*. He has written numerous books and has also made documentaries and written plays for radio and television. Having been a lifelong member of the Labour Party until 1988, he is now a member of Green Party.

THE MYTH
OF THE MARKET

Promises & Illusions

Jeremy Seabrook

GREEN
BOOKS

First published in 1990 by
Green Books
Ford House, Hartland
Bideford, Devon EX39 6EE

Photoset in 10 on 13½ pt Mergenthaler Ehrhardt
at Five Seasons Press, Madley, Hereford

Printed by Robert Hartnoll Ltd
Victoria Square, Bodmin, Cornwall

*Printed on Five Seasons
100 per cent recycled paper*

British Library Cataloguing in Publication Data
Seabrook, Jeremy, *1939–*
The Myth of the Market
1. Economics
I. Title
330

ISBN 1 870098 36 6

ACKNOWLEDGEMENTS

I should like to thank all those who have contributed to the making of this book, especially Winin Pereira, Nikhil Pereira, Gabriel Britto, Prema Gopalan, Mona Daswani and the women of SPARC, Vasant Jadhev, Anna Kurian, Achyut Deshpande, Vijay Kumar Anand, Vasudha and Celine of Maharashtra Prabodhan Seva Mandal; Marie Knox, Cathy and Tony McCormack, Pat and Katrina, Rodd Cherry, David and Alice Alexander; Clara Grilli, Gino Pogliazicci, Potenza, Celeste and Linda, Ali Hussein, Mustafa; Kyosti Urponen, Erik Arnkil; Ralph and Ellen Smith, Francis Irvin, Ruth Wantling, Carol Reitan, Lawrence Irvin, Terry Irvin, Donald Schoene, Sharon, Joe, Judy, Elaine Graybill, John English, Trevor Blackwell; and especially Derek Hooper.

London July 1989

CONTENTS

1 ⁄ THE MYTH OF THE MARKET

THE UNDISPUTED APPROVAL which the idea of the 'market economy' evokes in most people in the West, comes, at least in part, from the marriage of such a homely term as 'market' with the more exalted abstraction of 'economy'. What more universal and familiar image could be conjured up than that associated with the word 'market': the chaotic *souk*, the labyrinthine bazaar, the cobbled market-place with its primitive trestles, the streets of the old walled-city lined with vendors of fruit and vegetables, the cart-pullers and head-loaders with their pyramids of colourful produce, the romantic associations of Covent Garden or Les Halles. The idea of market extends from the breathtaking range of goods in Western hypermarkets to the pitiful offerings of a few over-ripe bananas or gourds in the dusty suburbs of the Third World city. Everything speaks of the local and the everyday, even when it is incorporated into the contradiction of a single, dominating 'global market'.

The positive connotations appear to express something so widespread and essential in human affairs that it places the market economy beyond contestation. It speaks of canny customers fingering the quality of cloth; turning over the produce to make sure that the best stuff hasn't been put on display while shoddier goods are hidden; sampling the merchandise before the judicious decision as to whether or not to make a purchase.

The very universality of buying and selling gains general acceptance: it is a deeply rooted activity in all societies. The beneficent image of market economy has been further enhanced by the malign consequences in those countries that have sought to interfere with its mysterious workings. The attempt to ban harmful or luxury products by some socialist societies has led only to a thriving black market. The story of East Europeans, hungry

9

for goods, offering Western tourists large sums of money for their watch, their jeans, their shoes, suggests irrepressible human needs and instincts that will be quelled by neither the most rigorous overseeing of bureaucrats nor the most vigilant endeavours of ideologues. The markets express something fundamental and unalterable: this is borne out by the words of historians like Fernand Braudel who, writing of towns, says, 'Wherever it may be, a town is inseparable from certain realities and processes, certain regular and recurring features. Where there is a town, there will be a division of labour, and where there is a marked division of labour, there will be a town. No town is without a market, and there can be no regional or national markets without towns. One hears a great deal about the role of the town in the development and diversification of consumption, but very little about the extremely important fact that even the humblest town-dweller must of necessity obtain his food supply through the market: the town, in other words, *generalizes* the market into a widespread phenomenon.'*

Markets, then, are universal mechanisms for answering human need, for bringing together buyers and sellers. Although they are morally neutral, many people have nevertheless seen in them both aesthetically satisfying symmetries and socially advantageous outcomes—the hidden hand that transmutes private purposes into public good. They are said to represent the most 'natural' means of matching human desires with the means of satisfying them. When we look at the energy and effort absorbed by buying and selling in the West, at the swiftness of the transactions, the accelerating circulation of money, the besieging of the shopping malls and *gallerias*, it is clear that something is occurring which goes far beyond a mere functional answering of need. We are in the presence of something more profound and significant.

Those people who maintain a lonely vigil on the cold pavements over Christmas in order not to lose sight of some coveted object in the sales; the paroxysm of spending that exhausts itself on Christmas Eve, only to be renewed two days later—on the day after Christmas, when the police have cordoned off some city-centres because they are saturated with traffic —indicate that we have long abandoned the prosaic and matter-of-fact

* Fernand Braudel, *On History*, (Weidenfeld & Nicolson, 1981)

activity implied by traditional definitions of the market. In the West, the buying of things (and indeed, services, experiences and sensations) has become inextricably bound up with the roots of human identity. We seek to express who we are through our purchases; and at this point, the process of buying and selling ceases to be a mere mechanism, but comes to give purpose, and even meaning, to our lives. What was an important aspect of all cultures has become the universalized focus of world culture. The market economy in the West, being the dominant force in the lives of the people, becomes a source, not only of well-being, but of morality; and in the absence of any other force that can match its power, it is looked to as a bringer of truth. In other words, the market economy has been not merely re-moralized in our time, but sanctified as it has never been before.

And indeed, the vigour, dynamism and energy of the market economy do make of it the most conspicuous and inescapable feature of our social lives. Its vitality commands respect; its very strength and salience predispose us to invest it with an extraordinary power. It is small wonder that it should have laid hold of both the imagination and the homeless faith of a majority of the people in the Western world. It has become the object of a quasi-religious cult.

For there are no secular societies in the world. All are held together by some deeply shared and transcendent faith. And the sacralizing of the market economy—or people's capitalism or the social market, or whatever other euphemisms its zealots have dreamed up to designate the capitalist system—has occurred in the absence of any other source of moral or religious authority in the rich Western societies. This is scarcely a new phenomenon; great strength and power have always been regarded by people as a sign that they have been favoured by divine providence; strength is readily interpreted as revelation.

We are confronted then, by a spiritual cult that has developed around what have always been considered purely material processes, and this latter fact serves only to shield from recognition the holy mysteries. Nowhere is the faith of the cult more ardently expressed than in that which unlocks access to limitless abundance and emancipation—money. Like all profound faiths, it is so widespread and unshakeable that it remains blind to all the noxious and baleful side-effects of its workings in the world: it does not see that the most basic human needs remain unanswered, and it coexists with the most grotesque excesses. Humanity continues to be ravaged, either by pitiful insufficiency or by debilitating superfluity.

We have only to glance at the financial pages of the newspapers and examine the language in which the money or commodities markets are described, to see at once to what degree these have been endowed with human, even superhuman characteristics. Markets are nervous or jittery, they are capricious or fickle, or they are more settled, calm. They are sensitive, hesitant or expectant. Market sentiment is anxiously sought; its verdict awaited, its response eagerly anticipated. Sometimes it sounds as though the language of chivalry were being deployed; at least, we are in the presence of patriarchal representations of woman. We learn that the pound sterling has had a good day, the dollar is ailing, the French franc is sinking fast—bulletins issued on the state of health of a dying monarch. If the markets have taken on human attributes, this is not simply an attempt to make comprehensible what are seen as unbiddable processes, but a mode of assimilating these to a force of nature, even a reflection of the divine will on earth.

At the same time, the language of the markets colonizes ever new areas of experience, reaching into what might have been regarded as the inviolable sanctuaries of the human heart. Do we not now talk of emotional investments, of the returns we get for our relationships? A psychic economics helps us judge whether other people are going to pay dividends, whether a friendship is profitless or rewarding, whether there is anything in it for us or whether it will cost us dear. Relationships become transactions; we shop around, or are in the market for a new affair or perhaps a long-term relationship, or even a one-night stand. Although our stock may be low, as long as we retain the assets of our looks or our brains, we can make capital out of them. We may get meagre returns for friendship, but on the other hand, there is always the unexpected bonus, the pay-off. The bottom line has invaded the recesses of our personal lives; and we all have our price.

In this reversal of humanity and the market, it becomes our business to appease the autonomous workings of an economic system, very much as so-called primitive societies seek to appease nature, in order to ensure that the crops flourish or the monsoon breaks at the appointed time. We have, it seems, increasingly robbed human beings of their qualities and ascribed them to the object of our worship, which then ceases to be lifeless and abstract. It is clear that in the West the economy has become a form of salvation; the realm of the economic is the only one in which miracles are now believed to occur by a cynical people; it performs, it delivers goods, it is a goose that lays golden eggs; religion, fable and fairy story are intertwined.

There are, perhaps, precise historical reasons for this development, which may be sought in the aftermath of the Second World War.* The speed and efficiency of the reconstruction of Europe after the ruin of 1945 came to be known as the *Wirtschaftswunder*. Its truly miraculous quality lay, perhaps, less in the prodigious material achievements than in its spectacular capacity to erase from our minds everything that had preceded it.

After the time of rubble and ashes, the charnel-house to which the cradle of civilization (as Europeans have been pleased to call their continent) had been reduced, the new era was to be a time of forgetting. Fascism, and the resulting war, far from appearing as the inevitable outcome of the poverty, depression and despair of the inter-war years, came to be presented as an aberration, a sombre—though eradicable—moment. If the rehabilitation of capitalism took precedence over everything else in 1945, this was only partially due to Europe's overriding need for material security for its tormented and exhausted people; it was also because the origins of the European conflagration had been all too apparent in the breakdown of the economic order of the twenties and thirties. In practice this meant that the economy became the focus, not simply of an endeavour to feed, clothe and house the people of the continent, but also of a version of salvation: an over-expiatory burden was placed upon the realm of economic activity that simply had no place there.

The economy became the arena in which the guilt for what had happened was to be assuaged. If it had been the faltering of the economy that had contributed to the unleashing of the horrors of the thirties and the war, it was the economy that must become the site and source of the pledge that no such thing would ever recur. In consequence, the economies of Western Europe became the object of a superstitious reverence: if only

---

* Some of this material also appears in *The Politics of Hope*, (Faber, 1988) —written with Trevor Blackwell, to whom I remain indebted.

13

these could be made to work, to grow, to provide, we would surely gain exemption from any recurrence of the barbarities of the recent past. They were charged with a sort of redemptive power; and their positioning at the centre of all political and moral concern, to the exclusion of everything else, in the 1950s and beyond, can be traced back to this moment of transfiguration.

That reconstruction took place in a context where the great humanitarian reforms of the welfare state were being negotiated, served only to obscure that what was being rebuilt were, in fact, the same edifices that had so spectacularly fallen into ruin. The establishment of the welfare state reinforced the certainty that there could be no going back, that mass poverty, unemployment and insecurity would never again be tolerated, let alone the atrocities that had come in their wake. But the structures of welfare were merely the scaffolding concealing the true architecture which was being restored with such loving care. It is no accident that the whole of Europe echoed to the busy sound of reconstructions, replicas, copies, of museum-like accuracy, of buildings that had been bombed or razed during the war: meticulously authentic *Schlosse*, intricately rebuilt cathedrals, medieval city centres, landmarks, palaces and piazzas, avenues lined with limes and chestnut-trees.

The luxuriant economic growth of the post-war years was fertilized with the corpses that lay in mass graves, marked and unmarked, all over Europe, in the sense that it represented an attempt to undo what was irreversible, to escape the consequences and to set a distance between ourselves and the enormity we had lived through. If the period had a feverish quality, this came perhaps from the suppression of a decent interval of mourning; its busy-ness betrayed a rejection of responsibility, its eager activity spoke of denial. In order to avoid any real atonement, or even reflection, all energies were thrown into the work of economic renewal; and by the mid-fifties, all memory of what had gone before seemed to have been expunged from the popular consciousness. It is not a coincidence that the eighties saw a resurgence of Nazi-hunting; frail elderly men taken out of their hiding-place in South America, arraigned on charges of torture and mass murder, their old age seeming to dissimulate a monstrous and barely credible evil. It was a belated, indeed impossible attempt to do the necessary work that was avoided then.

These elisions and evasions were served only too well by the Cold War, for it permitted us to project onto our enemies in Eastern Europe the guilt for an inhumanity which capitalism *in extremis* had given rise to in the thirties. Because the socialist countries were indeed responsible for the cruelties with which they were charged, they became a ready psychological dumping-ground for the wrongs committed by the West also, a suitable resting-place for the toxic waste of our hatreds. As a result, the capitalism of the post-war era stood before us, wonderfully cleansed, free of impurities, untainted by buried scandals.

During the 1950s and 1960s, this task of regenerating capitalism and its thorough moral rehabilitation went unchallenged in mainstream politics. Those who raised the faintest whisper of criticism against what came to be called the consumer society met with disproportionate anger, denial and resentment; with the result that any questioning of its workings provoked the kind of denunciation traditionally attracted by blasphemy, an attack upon the sacred. Few at that time doubted that the violent and wasteful distortions of what was serenely regarded as economic progress were anything but benign. Its purpose had already become far removed from simply transactions supplying the needs of the people, but had become an object of extreme veneration, the source of all hope. Those who criticized were called, at best, puritans and killjoys; it was snobbish and élitist to speak of any restriction on the spread of good things. 'Why shouldn't the people be given what they want?' was the most conclusive argument, advanced most vociferously by those who, in the past, had spared nothing to demonstrate why the people should be deprived, not only of what they wanted, but of the very necessities for their survival. No slur must be cast upon the shining innocence of a social and economic endeavour that now appeared in the world in the guise of deliverer of the people. Indeed, it exuded a promise of social redemption, a grandiose claim formerly restricted to the representatives of certain versions of socialism. This act of piracy, whereby the claims that socialism alone could transform the world were usurped by capitalism, helped to turn capitalism into a semi-religious cult.

In this way, economic performance came to be the measure by which all social, moral and spiritual well-being was to be judged. Political debate, as was to be expected, shrank in the presence of such an awesome phenomenon to discussions as to which party could make the economy work most efficiently. This preoccupation superseded and cancelled all other concerns. That many European socialist parties embraced this enterprise with enthusiasm, attaching their fortunes, in an historic wager, to the probability that the capacity for growth of the capitalist economies was infinite, had much to do with the crisis of socialism in the eighties.

Unhappily, the savour of death which had accompanied this particular rebirth became absorbed by the neo-colonial order of the post-war world, whereby the ostensibly independent countries of an older empire were locked into subordination to patterns of development required by the West for maintenance of its miracle. Just as the bones of the European dead had fed the urgent energies of economic reconstruction, so, in more recent times, poverty, hunger, avoidable disease and death in the Third World became the daily tribute to those omnivorous, indeed cannibalistic, processes. If we find ourselves disarmed and impotent in the presence of some of their consequences now—the destruction of nature, upon which all economic systems rest, the depletion of resources, the poisoning of the earth—this is partly because it is no easy task to dismantle and desacralize that which for so long has been the repository of our faith and the source of all hope.

The guilt left by the Second World War, in which the appeasers and conciliators of fascism, no less than its apologists and enthusiasts, have their share, could not be allayed in the ways we sought. This is why, as the refurbished façades crack, the showy surface glitter fades, we can see once more the form of ghosts which were never laid, but remained dormant, waiting to be roused up from the shallow graves which had been trampled so indecently in the rush to rebuild. Through the peeling paint, the stained cement and the desolate concrete, the landscaped terrain of the cities, we can clearly discern the contours of that which laid waste the continent in 1945; not only poverty and unemployment, insecurity and fear, but the accumulation of vast armouries of devastation, and above all, the racism and in-turned nationalisms that thrive on people's feelings of impotence and helplessness. The racism of Western Europe is more than colonial nostalgia. The migrants, the blacks, the *Gastarbeiter*, the Mahgrebans are human hostages to global patterns of inequality and exploitation, both the symbols and living consequences of a Third World systematically ravaged and distorted for the sake of the sacred expanding economy of the West. They are the reproach, not simply to an imperial past, but equally to the rapacious present of a system in which the sacrifice of human flesh has been a central rite ever since it first made its bloody and ruthless appearance in the world.

As the fabric of the restored economy grows more threadbare, we have no choice but to underwrite its continued expansion in the monstrous coalescence into the single European market: we must sustain the act of faith made in the early years of reconstruction and worked out in the subsequent half century. Fear binds us to the increasingly unlikely hope that growth will continue for ever, no matter what deformed and cancerous tissue it may generate, no matter how penetrated by the smell of death which it brings, or has brought, to numberless though invisible others, distant from us in time, like the European war dead, or in space, like the poor yielding their last breath within sight of unparalleled global plenty.

If we had been a little wiser, we might have understood that even though the breakdown of economic order can certainly bring ruin and desolation, nevertheless economics is not a vehicle of redemption. It is now clear that the purpose of the post-war period was not about the saving of humanity, but rather the salvation of capitalism.

And saved it assuredly was; through those reforms which re-shaped people's lives, reforms that have since grown threadbare, revealing once more that nature of what was saved.

2/ THE MYTH OF WELFARE

IN THE CELEBRATED PARAGRAPH 565 of the Beveridge Report, the document which above all inspired the founding of the welfare state in Britain, Lord Beveridge identified 'five Giant evils'. These were Want, Disease, Ignorance, Squalor and Idleness; and the means whereby these were to be eliminated were then set forth. The 1945 Labour government duly achieved what was thought to be necessary to lay to rest, once and for all, these scourges of the poor.

In the eighties, it became clear during the process of economic restructuring that these Giants were by no means eradicated. They may have been transformed, metamorphosed even, but they have not gone away. They have adapted themselves to the existence of the welfare state, and have re-emerged with greater audacity in our time; not always in the same guise, it is true, but modified in ways that fit the altered landscape of our lives. They blend more appropriately with the decor of what is sometimes—tendentiously—described as post-industrial society. Their re-appearance raises the disturbing possibility that they remain the necessary and inseparable attendants of a system that defies all the attempts of reformers to destroy them. They may be less easy to recognize in the new forms they have assumed; but their presence is unmistakable, a blighting and destructive force in the lives of those who were to have been delivered from them for ever.

Most people would have little difficulty in acknowledging the recurrence of Idleness. Mass unemployment, felt for a long time to be politically intolerable, has proved remarkably acceptable, not only to those securely in work, but equally to large numbers of those required to offer themselves as sacrificial victims to the regeneration of capitalism. And in addition to conventional ideas of worklessness, who can count the numbers of people drawn into demeaning and unsatisfying labour that does violence to their abilities and diminishes their talents? Who could describe the noxious in-utilities for the sake of which the energies of the young have been appropriated? What forms of ill-rewarded and repressive under-employment weigh on the spirit and dull the mind of a new generation of workers?

As for Want, that certainly exists, with more than seven million people dependent upon the state for their income. The common wisdom is that, like unemployment, want has been much mitigated by welfare provision. This assumption takes little account of the lived experience of contemporary unemployment and modernized poverty. Far from being assuaged by welfare, they have been aggravated by a context of insistent and aggressive images of plenty, by a culture which ceaselessly advertises its desire to shower its bounty upon the people. The Child Poverty Action Group in Britain expressed its concern recently at the difficulty in bringing home to people the curiously harrowing pressures of present-day poverty: the charity could not find an image that would adequately convey the feeling. This was scarcely surprising, for the great majority of images (and images are what this society specializes in, appearances and surfaces) are of remorseless luxury and overwhelming plenty. The omnipresence of such scenes of comfort and ease only reinforce the idea that those who fail to avail themselves of their share of the eager capitalist cornucopia must, in some way, be defective individuals. It must be their own fault. Pictures of poverty are easily eclipsed and overlaid by images of well-being. Indeed, the latter are ideology materialized. They tell us that poverty and unemployment are not flaws in the system, but the problems of individuals. The implication is that there are no longer any socially-determined evils; only faulty people. The rewards and prizes are so insistently tangible that those cut off from them must be deficient indeed. It is all of a piece with the sanctification of the social and economic order.

What of the other horrors which Beveridge sought to banish? Surely they have been effectively dealt with. Disease, for instance. If there is one thing the West can be proud of, it is the advance in medical care; the reduction of infant mortality, the elimination of TB, the cure of formerly fatal disorders, the enhanced life-expectancy. That these old afflictions have gone is plain for all to see. But it may be that the continuities are to be found elsewhere—perhaps in the sicknesses of addiction, the self-induced damage, the maladies of excess. It is significant that, in the mid-eighties, the Lord Chief Justice, adverting to the problem of heroin in Britain, said that it was 'worse than cholera or typhoid'; and at a British Medical Association conference, a psychiatrist said that heroin addiction is 'not an epidemic now, it is a plague'. Subsequently, the same thing was said about cocaine, and then crack. We sometimes talk in metaphors that give us a strong sense of ugly recurrences, correspondences that seem to repeat the evils of the first industrial era. We refer to 'outbreaks of violence', 'epidemics' of crime. In one area, there has been a 'rash' of outrages against the elderly; elsewhere 'waves' of attacks on Asians; racial incidents 'flare up'. The riots of the early eighties, the destructiveness of youthful drinkers in country towns later in the decade, were felt to have been intensified by a 'copy-cat' effect; in other words, they were contagious. It is in the emergence of such phenomena that the samenesses persist, in spite of the ostensible transformation of the system. The consequences of contemporary diseases are the same as those left by earlier visitations; a young person destroyed by glue or drugs, or left bleeding to death on a suburban pavement after a knifing at a party, suffers no less than those who went to paupers' graves in the cholera epidemics of the early nineteenth century. The fevers of today take their toll in stress, heart disease, and cancers—one in three people in Britain has, or will suffer from, cancer. Indeed, the removal of earlier forms of sickness only makes way for new ones, many of them self-inflicted. One in five hospital beds in Britain is occupied by people suffering from alcohol-related illness. It is perhaps not an accident that the resurrection of these evils—or perhaps reincarnation would be a more accurate expression—should have been accompanied by the revivalist rhetoric of the eighties; the years of Thatcher and Reagan, with their belief in the Second Coming of Political Economy or laissez-faire, or whatever fervours inspired their graveyard evangelism. The deep cultural resonances of the rhetoric of fundamentalism, the return to our roots, Victorian values, lie in the eerie impression that we have somehow been revisiting the first industrial epoch, in spite of all the glittering, refurbished appearances.

Ignorance, too, seems an unlikely characteristic of 'information-rich' societies, where there have been so many people busily 'communicating' with each other. But the spread of industries based upon 'information'—that enclosing and appropriation of knowledge—depends, for its success, on the manufacture of ignorance, on a special kind of unknowing. The advertising industry, for instance, contrary to its own claims that it teaches and informs, is in the business of the creation of an ignorance that is functionally essential in the consumer economies of the West. For one thing, its insistence upon the value and desirability of the commodity or service spirits away all concern with its origin, content, the suffering involved in its production and the consequences of its sale. The purpose of advertising is to sanctify all purchases, any purchases. It sacralizes all transactions of buying and selling, blesses the act of acquisition with the noise and show and excitement it generates around each fresh marketed item. A cloud of unknowing envelopes the mysterious communion between vendor and buyer, conjuring away all the awkward questions, such as whose mouths have been denied food to furnish succulent milk-fed chickens or corn-fed beef to supermarket shoppers; or who might have been dispossessed of the land where women once grew food for subsistence, ousted for the sake of out-of-season fruits and vegetables exported to the West; or who might have been driven by landlessness to leave the home village, walk two hundred miles for the privilege of work in a sweat-shop to produce some fashionable export garment destined to be tomorrow's rags; or who has crawled underground in a mine guarded by the military to fetch out the metal that will be shaped into some trifling ornament. Ignorance, not, this time, in the sense of antique superstitious awe at the vagaries of the natural world which must be propitiated by ritual and magic, but a kind of licensed unknowing, a dissociative collusion that disengages the sovereign consumer from any responsibility towards those who produce. Indeed, it is possible to discern in these processes the re-creation of a kind of artificial peasantry, as remote from the things they buy as peasants subservient to the mysteries of nature. This modernized form of ignorance is not incompatible with people being better informed than ever before; such ignorance is a carefully wrought artefact, admirable in its impermeability to moral and ethical instruction.

And what of Squalor? The dismantling of the 'classic' industrial structures of the nineteenth century, the slums and tenements, mills and factories, was to have abolished those cruel sites of a suffering indelibly fixed by Victorian observers and reformers. But this has proved to be the most superficial and cosmetic landscaping of capitalism. The squalors of contemporary life are not to be found in the infested interiors, with their orange-box furniture, sacking at the window, the empty cupboard, dry crust and guttering candle; nor even in the mephitic breath of open drains and offal-strewn canals. We are looking at other forms of pollutant, the less visible destroyers of the human body: radiation, nitrates in the water supply, contaminants in the food-chain, the unrecognized toxins in value-added, nutrient-depleted foods, the undetected carcinogens in the industrial processes. There are other squalors too: a stream of ugly graffiti on concrete walls and pedestrian underpasses, denouncing alkies and poofs and wankers; the sagas of disgrace and violence, gloatingly chronicled by the popular and local press—the violation of women, abuse of children, the ruined relationships and vulnerable attachments of human beings; the sordid output of a misnamed entertainment industry, where any evening's television viewing will yield a sequence of people being mangled, murdered and blasted apart, and of the sex industry, where the youth and beauty of women are driven to market like any other commodity. In contrast with the fervours and ecstasies generated by the advertising of things, a ruined humanity haunts popular discourse in the form of muggers, addicts, child-molesters, rapists, brutes, fiends, vandals, wreckers, scroungers, loonies and psychopaths. This cultural and ideological sewage has its effect upon our lives in ways which appear so different from, yet which remain evocative of the fetid overflow of the stagnant and poisoned canals of Engels' Manchester.* For all the change of scenery, old patterns impose themselves: the lineaments of Beveridge's Giant evils have been modified, re-worked in the beautified surfaces, but the ugly familiar shapes are still discernible, transformed by the effects of a shallow welfarism, but essentially intact.

And how would it have been possible that these Giants should not survive? They are indispensable in a society in which the perpetuation of poverty and its grisly attendants is of primordial importance. Poverty remains essential to the purposes of capitalism, with its archaic promise of

---

* Friedrich Engels, *Condition of the Working Class in England, 1845,* (Allen & Unwin, London, 1968)

economic growth instead of sufficiency, not because the resources are lacking to provide for the people, but for ideological reasons. There is no want of the wherewithal to provide enough for everyone; but there is an overriding need that people should feel constantly impoverished, pauperized in ways that will goad them into seeking afresh some remedy in the capitalist version of riches. Without the spur of cruel, renewed and debilitating poverties, we might be content to rest in the security that there is enough for all—not only for the people in the rich world, but for those suffering more absolute want in the Two-Thirds World. If poverty really had been mitigated, rendered less degrading and brutal an experience, all the relentless striving might be seen for the driven, tormented absurdity that it is. That poverty does not have to be a dehumanizing experience may be seen in the elective poverty of a monastery or in the practice of subsistence societies. It is clear that market economies, by their very nature, create poverty of a very different order—one which appears to have its remedy in the plethora of commodities and services which are their reason for existence. That no such remedy may be found there is demonstrated by the continued dissatisfactions and impoverishments even among the richest and most favoured. Indeed, curing poverty is not their purpose at all, for poverty is not a sickness of the market economies, but evidence of its robust health.

3/ DISSECTING THE SOCIAL MARKET ECONOMY

THERE HAVE BEEN curious and unforeseeable consequences of the marriage of welfare with capitalism; the result has been a strange mutation, one which has taken on a life and dynamic of its own. But the spectres of the classic moment of capitalism still haunt this new creation, elusive yet familiar, unchanged, yet altered beyond recognition; and they continue their work of impoverishment and loss, as they did then.

That the welfare state came as a blessing to the vast majority of the people remains beyond dispute; that it proved to be the proudest achievement of social democracy is equally clear. But its precise contribution to the economic and social system—the worst rigours of which it was designed to palliate—remained, for a long time, ambiguous. Certainly, without the welfare state, politicians would never have ventured to talk about 'caring capitalism' or the 'social market'. For all those right-wing arguments about the moral fibre of the nation having been undermined, of feather-bedding and softening up, it has proved no easy task to dismantle the welfare system. Even Mrs Thatcher and Ronald Reagan, as eager to release market forces as any liberators of caged songbirds, were compelled to leave the substance intact; Mrs Thatcher, in particular declared again and again that the health service was safe in her—in other contexts—less than merciful hands.

The welfare state appeared in the 1940s as a profoundly liberating force to millions of people whose lives had been shadowed by fear of doctors' bills, the workhouse and a pauper's grave. That it depended absolutely on the wealth created by the continuing growth and expansion of capitalism did not then appear to be a disadvantage; and in any case, capitalism became transmuted during the 1950s, through a terminological concession by social democracy, into 'the economy'. In Britain, Anthony Crosland's book *The Future of Socialism* explicitly tied the Labour Party in perpetuity to what then seemed the infinitely extensible powers of growth of the capitalist endeavour; and the welfare state was admitted to be subordinate to the fortunes of the very economic system which the Labour Party came into being, if not to supersede, at least significantly to humanize.

What Mrs Thatcher's efforts to rehabilitate the immutable laws of political economy did in the eighties was to illuminate clearly the hybrid that had been formed by the coming together of the welfare state and the market economy: these two apparently separate—and in some versions, warring—phenomena merged, to create an organic whole, a new kind of society, which took on an autonomous existence from which neither component could be easily isolated.

For one thing, without the structures of welfare, the vast regeneration of capitalism in the post-war period would have been unthinkable: pop culture, the industries devoted to entertainment, style and fantasy could never have gained the pre-eminence they have if the people had remained prey to hunger, want and insecurity. At their most extreme, malnutrition and high fashion are not happy companions: the essence of the apparent starvelings who model clothes in the West is that theirs is a willed, not involuntary emaciation. The blending of the market economy with the health, beauty and well-being of the post-war generations created a symbiotic and inextricable unity. In spite of the rhetoric of neo-liberals in the 1980s, the achievement of Mrs Thatcher's 'reforming'—even 'radical'—administrations will, in the long term, be seen to have been more limited; the modification of the existing arrangements far less extensive than some of the hyberbole might suggest. For they have by no means demolished the welfare state. It is true that the poor and the unemployed have been subjected to what some might see as a salutary turn of the screw, but these are a minority, and a divided and confused electoral force. It is true that an agreeably abrasive edge of insecurity has been re-inserted into everyday life, an aggravated anxiety; but for all that, the apparatus of caring has remained, more or less, in place.

There is no doubt that the Conservatives in Britain long to go further. But one result of the singular alloy of the market economy with welfare has been not only the profound interdependence of the two, but an equal dependency upon both in the people who have grown up in the material conditions thus created. So when the critics on the right declare that the welfare state has undermined the creativity and independence of people, their assertion is not entirely baseless; and when the left points to the distortions of the markets, the production of wasteful and injurious superfluities while so many basic needs remain unanswered, the truth of such observations is not easily denied. But both criticisms, in the presence of intractable reality, sound more and more ritualistic; institutionalised formulae, fine for ideological feast-days, but unlikely to influence the way we live.

The new hybrid—caring capitalism—becomes peculiarly unresponsive to further modification and reform. It should not surprise us that the interdependence of welfare and markets should produce in the people all the symptoms of dependency—enslavement to technology, 'progress' or a rising income; addictions, whether to permitted or forbidden drugs, from crack to alcohol; obsessive reliance upon work or leisure, escapism, constant entertainment, over-stimulation, and above all, thraldom to money, which alone can sustain the life-support system, and which turns out to be the most dangerously addictive substance known to humankind. These things are the far from benign consequences of reforms and efforts at improvement which, although they could perhaps not have been foreseen at the time when welfare and markets coalesced, cannot be ignored now. This is how fundamentalists of both right and left are partly in error and partly correct in their diagnosis of those apparently irremediable ills of our time, which everyone acknowledges and deplores, but to which few feel able to propose precise cures.

This is why those political groups who oppose the ideology of industrial growth for its own sake strike, not only at the barbarities of the market-system, but also against the machinery of a welfare which depends upon it. When the Greens advocate an alternative-growth society, another economic accounting-system, they expose themselves to the accusation that they are, at the same time, undermining the well-being of the people, to which they profess so strong an attachment. In this context, the Conservatives find themselves in the unfamiliar role of champions and defenders of the poor of the earth (in much the same way that they became the unlikely supporters of the working class in the West): why should we deny the benefits we enjoy, they virtuously proclaim, to the poor? They thus show themselves as antagonists of the Greens, advocates of a world development that simply replicates what has happened in the West all over the globe. In this confusion, political discussion melts into mere words, pieties and incantations. It seems impossible to attack one aspect of the way we live, without the rest of it unravelling, threatening to melt into chaos and incoherence.

Those who seek a way towards a new politics must, if their claims are to be believed, offer an alternative, not only to existing patterns of growth in industrial society, but also to that particular version of welfare that has grown up as a parasitic development upon it. This would mean unpicking the whole compromise between capital and labour, that fusion of cradle-to-grave welfarism of social democracy in the 1940s and the capitalist response to it, in the shape of the consumer society in the 1950s. For everything that has happened since then has been the working out of the interaction of these two elements. One result of this is that if present forms of economic growth were to be interrupted, welfare would also atrophy; and this would represent a double disaster, too terrible to contemplate.

What it means is that a genuinely contestatory politics would have to offer other models of welfare, which would be in harmony with those other models of economic development now being formulated. This is not an impossible project; simply one that will require courage and vision and imagination, and indeed, much else that has been absent for so long from our lives. For that other version of welfare, detached from the infinitely expanding economy, would be one in which people care for each other in non-monetary and non-professionalized ways. Caring would cease to be a function of the markets, the purposes of which are to be for ever creating new ways for us to spend the money which we are so busy making that it becomes impossible for us to devote the attention necessary to the welfare of each other. There would also be a very different health service from that dominated by spectacular technology designed to repair the broken well-being and injured spirit of the time—much of it inflicted by the violence that attends the creation of wealth; a health service that would seek to anticipate, indeed, to forestall such damage. That this cannot be accomplished through reform should by now be obvious, for it would involve a reconstruction of our whole lives. If we are to look for release from the paralysis, the individual powerlessness and all the expensively structured discontents which have been the inescapable outcome of that bonding between welfare and capitalism, we must seek it in the language and practice of liberation. Increasingly, the welfare state is servicing an untenable and expensive value-added unhappiness of 'advanced' industrial society—advanced, it seems increasingly, only on the road to self-destruction.

That a truly radical path cannot be followed by any of the mainstream political parties which remain tethered to one or other part of this formidable construct, may be read in the efforts of left and right to deal with the issues that fall within the 'competence' of the other. For instance, when social democracy makes an audacious sortie into the territory normally appropriated by the right—law and order, drugs and violence—the targets are well-chosen; but the only specific proposed to an eager Labour Party conference turns out to be more policemen on the beat, better street lighting, the employment of more customs officers, the 'security' of yet more bolts and locks and chains on doors and windows—the most superficial kind of public spending to which Labour hitched its destiny long ago. It simply fails to respond to the urgency with which people feel. Just as Mrs Thatcher is left with a welfare state she may secretly deplore but cannot dismember, so Labour dare not look closely at the causes of violence, addiction and despair, because it might discover that these are written into the imperatives of the market economy which it has long ceased to contest.

The compromise of 1945, which was to have transformed European society, did its work. A transformation did occur; only the outcome and consequences were not foreseeable. But nothing remains still: the hybrid created then has pursued its own, sometimes perverse, trajectory through time, and we are confronted by effects never anticipated then. To pretend that these can be dealt with within the structures and institutions in place has been the object of nearly all political endeavour in our time; a fiction which has merely deferred the moment of recognition. In the meantime, while false polarities, unreal opposites and partial contradictions continue to be the object of sterile and exhausted debate, the visions of how an alternative society might be realized are hard to sustain. It is the vital task of radical politics to retrieve and animate these visions, to show that there are ways out of the present impasse, which so de-powers people, creates such frustration, impotence and cynicism. That the need for such emancipatory movements has not been answered by even the best efforts of labourism is now clear.

There is a significant core of people in Britain, as elsewhere in the West, who have grown into adult life as dependants of the welfare state. They have come through childhood on what was national assistance, later supplementary benefit, now income support, into adult unemployment, and have now brought up their own children in the same circumstances. The conditions in which such people live are familiar, not only to social workers, but to any viewer of those television documentaries of which they have so often been the subject: the hard-to-let housing estates, the rank grass and half-wild dogs, the broken windows and burgled meters, the jumble-sale clothes and Social Services Department furniture, second-hand cookers and stained foam mattresses; 'existing, not living' as they will tell you. Whether the consistent aggravation of their position by the actions of the Conservative government in the eighties derived from its detestation of the poor or its loathing of the welfare state may be disputed; but their experience has been of worsening hardship and intensified pressure.

All the arguments about welfare dependency have been ceded to the right. The left has found it difficult to concede that any such issue exists, and has accordingly proscribed the topic, surrounded it by a political taboo, which is the way with ideology when confronted by awkward realities that jar against its revelations. And yet, there is something both upsetting and disturbing about dependency upon the caring agencies of the state (the benign effects of which are increasingly being counteracted, if not nullified, by its multiplying agencies of coercion). This is not to suggest that there is anything morally bracing about leaving the poorest to fend for themselves, to make their own accommodation with unemployment, disability and death: this will merely fill the towns and cities with beggars, as any visitor to the cities of the Third World immediately becomes aware.

It isn't even that the impenetrable and labyrinthine workings of the welfare system itself are the source of its inefficacy (although these are certainly no help either); nor does it originate with their often ill-paid and resentful custodians and administrators (although their understandable ill-will also contributes little). What makes life on welfare so cruel—and it is a different kind of cruelty from that in societies where there is no welfare provision at all— is the context in which the system of relief must operate, and the values that dominate it. For dependency on welfare is only a more naked and intensive version of over-extending and more total reliance on money, an institutionalising of a wider dependency in the rich industrial societies. It is not welfare, but the growing, and, it seems, boundless, power of money, the increasing trust in it and what it can buy that is the true agent of dispossession, the real source of the loss of autonomy and independence in people. This is what more and more constrains human—as opposed to entrepreneurial—initiative, stifles creativity, extinguishes imagination, and directs growing areas of activity through the narrowing filter of the markets. The spoiling, the de-grading and exclusion of the freely-given, the mutually exchanged, of all the things and services we offer each other spontaneously and without cost, leads to a slow shrinkage of the non-monetized realm of social intercourse.

It is a commonplace in the critique of conventional economics that this measures only the cash-transactions of the official market economy: all private sector production, employment, consumption, investment and savings; all state and local government expenditure and income. That this is supported by a cash-based 'underground economy' is also recognized. But all this, in turn, rests upon the non-monetized 'counter-economy', as the economist Hazel Henderson calls it, which subsidizes the GNP sector with unpaid labour, do-it-yourself, bartering, social, family and community structures, unpaid household work, parenting, voluntary work, sharing, mutual aid, caring for the majority of the old and the sick, home-based production for use, subsistence agriculture. All of this, of course, is sustained in turn by the natural-resource base, which absorbs many of the costs of the official economy, as well as many of those of the counter-economy. What all this indicates is that official economic systems are far less comprehensive, less complete structures than they have claimed to be.

What we have lived through in the rich world has been the accelerating passage of non-monetized activity into the formal economy, its colonization by market transactions. Being on welfare simply illuminates the extent to which the poorest have also been penetrated by this dominant process (and market-penetration is precisely what the ugly jargon suggests, a violation). For the poor, the last penny is accounted for before it even reaches their hands, for shelter, food, heating and clothing. The sense of impotence in the presence of money all used up in advance is what makes of welfare such a shaming and unfree experience. In societies in which freedom is increasingly reduced to the meaning of freedom to spend, it is only to be expected that the poor will feel their liberties curtailed to the point of violent constriction. The poor, more than anyone else, feel the limitations of lives in which all human abilities are in the process of being superseded by the supreme ability—to go shopping. Such developments can occur only in societies where a majority of the people have access to a rising disposable income: the rich must always find more and more ingenious things on which to spend their money. The degree to which this leaves the poor stranded, set apart, cut off, cannot be exaggerated: theirs is a state of dependent exclusion.

Here, we are close to the heart of the Green critique. What could be more prodigal and wasteful than the vast expenditure of human energy in the effort to sell more and more things to people, the need for which had not previously occurred to them? Not only does this dynamic process hasten the depletion of world resources, but it also crushes and stifles the human resources which people have deployed in living successful and self-reliant lives, without some of the excesses which have suddenly become indispensable.

One of the reasons why so many young people in the West leave school able neither to deal with the institutions of the society that shelters them, nor to respond to some of its most elementary demands, is not because they have been the victims of idle or permissive teachers, but because their understanding and curiosity have been not aroused but quenched, by the superior knowledge of what money can buy, and without which, as they will readily tell anyone who asks, you can do nothing; as though money itself had become the sole key and motor of all human activity. In the United States, it is estimated that functional illiteracy is now at thirty per cent. If this is so, it is because buying and selling have become the site where action, invention and creativity are extinguished. The decay of human possibilities is inscribed in the very structures of the market economy with its dilating range of monetary possibilities. This may help to explain the increase in violence and crime in those societies as they get richer, a development which some commentators and observers claim to be puzzled by. In the United States in 1988, there were thirty-eight million crimes, including 20,000 murders. Far from being 'mindless', as it is called in the denunciations of all kinds of conservatives, such violence is an ugly but understandable response to processes of expropriation and loss beyond the simple absence of material necessities; it is an expression of the extinction of social hope, of the death of any alternative remedy to their despair other than acts of individual plunder.

The intensifying monetization of our lives has one vast advantage to our rulers. As we become more dependent on money, we feel more depowered without it, and are thus more prey to terror at the thought of change or loss of what we have. Our vaunted 'standard of living' is a kind of life-support system, which in fact indicates very little about the *level* at which we live, but everything about the way in which we live: it is essentially an index of pecuniary penetration. It scarcely matters what we buy, or what adulterations or contaminants accompany our purchases. Faith in the rising income attaches us securely to a market-place which we rely upon to prompt, inspire, suggest to us how to spend our money. In other words, the market-place becomes the focus of all increase and enlargement in our lives. This renders us all the more amenable to manipulation and control; a development which affords immense satisfaction to those set above us, who are delighted to discover that they no longer have to turn the police and the military against the people to ensure their compliance with the immutable laws of political economy. In the elegant imagery of contemporary politics, the carrot has replaced the stick; an image whose banality and associations convey precisely the opinion of those whose high calling it is to keep us in our place. Perhaps this is why the freedom to buy more and more things is inexorably becoming a surrogate for all our other lost liberties, and the overriding objective of those societies which are pleased to call themselves democratic.

A radical politics would look at ways, not of deepening our subordination to the cash economy, but of seeking our release, where possible, from it. It would propose a programme of reclamation of all that we can offer each other without the mediation of money; would seek to regain as many freely exchanged services and commodities as possible; would rediscover the numberless delights and distractions with which we can amuse and entertain each other, the functions and purposes we can provide for ourselves and one another by liberating these from the captivity of the markets. It would create demonetized zones of human endeavour. The question, for instance, of paying for labour that has traditionally been performed by women for nothing would become a question of a more equitable sharing of that work, not of getting it priced in the market-place. The process of assessing the cost of things is infinite: already we know how much money is required to pay for adequate care of the elderly or children; how long will it be before the value of a love-affair is calculated, before the price of human affections is known, what the going rate is for emotional security or acts of love? Already one hears people solemnly declare that they cannot afford to have another child, in the way that they regret not being able to afford a new car or an extra holiday.

The issue is not so much one of going 'beyond' the market economy, but rather of reducing it to a minimal, functional level in our lives, putting it in its (necessary) place. At present, it is allowed free passage into deeper and deeper places in the heart, imagination and spirit of people. By resisting this process, we might well discover areas of autonomy, independence and inventiveness that have been put to sleep through our automatic surrender to the invasion of a dispossessing enrichment, a pauperizing wealth, which we have come to accept as part of a 'natural' process. The greatest lesson might be, not how little we can achieve without a lot of money, but how much we can accomplish with relatively little.

The projection onto welfare of a major disabling influence on people's lives has gone unchallenged; it serves as a useful diversion from the true source of that which makes us feel subjectively poorer even while our material riches accumulate. Because the alternative to the market economy appears so bleak—that of state planning, the clumsy mechanisms that have failed the people in existing socialist societies—this does not therefore mean that the market economy is perfect, and beyond critical scrutiny. Yet this is what has happened. One of the great tragedies of Gorbachev's efforts to reform the Soviet system lies, not so much in the difficulty he has had in implementing them, as in the way they have been interpreted by Western politicians, ever eager to juxtapose socialist error against capitalist truth. In the sublime mission of rehabilitating the market economy, they have sought to occlude the space that might have opened up between the two warring world-systems. The West has represented change in the Soviet Union as repentance: it has been seen as the first move towards the reabsorption of the heretical creed of socialism into the bosom of the true church of orthodox political economy. This home-coming, the return of this prodigal is a time for festive rejoicing indeed. It also marks the passage of the famous dictum 'There is no alternative', from the domestic into the global arena. No wonder the flags are out to welcome back those who had strayed into the darker reaches of ideology, those blind alleys of history. Nothing will be spared in the high purpose of adding lustre and virtue to the market system. It is thus proclaimed the surest guarantor of our liberties, the finest ornament of Western (and hence, world) civilization. Everything conspires to place it beyond the reach of criticism, at a time when what we should be saying is that beyond a certain level, the extension of market transactions into human lives becomes damaging, corrosive and destructive; and this before we even begin to survey the effects of this industrialization of our humanity upon the natural base of the earth. Instead of veneration for money, we ought to be devising ways in which we could be delivered from the more baleful effects of its imperatives. They might be quite modest ways at first. What kind of simple things might be protected from monetary transactions? Perhaps the instruction and amusement of children without all the elabor-ate apparatus and equipment which we have been persuaded are essential to the most elementary learning processes; perhaps talking to each other rather than spending the five or six hours a day which the average Amer-ican dedicates to the watching of television, turned away from living flesh and blood; resisting the latest object of promotion and avoiding thereby the inevitable subsequent disappointment; perhaps celebrating and sing-ing our own lives, rather than those of mega-stars and super-heroes who can never be more than phantoms and shadows in our experience.

Those freedoms which begin and end with disposable income are always controlled by the rich, who have defined the terms on which they are conceded. And because there is apparently no limit to the needs, satis-factions and consolations which can be marketed (all of Hazel Hender-son's counter-economy will pass that way unless we resolve to prevent it), no individual can ever gain enough money to purchase them all. That is why even the richest can be heard complaining about all the things they cannot afford. When everything is for sale, we want everything, and yet we still want for so many things. In the rich Western societies wants have been sent to war against need. Security, sufficiency, mutuality remain elusive and unattainable, for they are not to be found in the realm of monetary satisfactions. Perhaps this is why we turn instead to those things that can be obtained for money. Our disturbed and agitated plunder of what we can buy becomes not only a search for what we want, but also a compensatory impulse for all the things we cannot have. The market-place, it seems, is less of a monument to the infinite elasticity of desire than to all the needs that must remain unfulfilled because they cannot be assuaged in this, the only permitted locus of human expression. Commodity substitution for our deepest yearnings is a profanation of our humanity; and this, if we have ears to listen, is what the poor of both North and South, are trying to say.

4 / THE IDEOLOGY OF COMMON SENSE

THE REHABILITATION OF CAPITALISM has been possible only because of its vastly augmented capacity to produce, and to provide the majority of people in the West with those necessities of life which it had, in an earlier epoch, so conspicuously withheld. That relief from poverty is a desirable objective is not in dispute: this, after all, is what most people have wanted above all else through recorded history. What we must ask is on what terms has the end of gross material deprivation been granted in the rich Western societies and what are the consequences of that particular endeavour to answer human need. This may appear to be cavilling at the spectacular improvements of the mid- and late-twentieth century, yet in fact, such a question goes to the root of the Green critique.

It will not escape attentive observers that individuals are only too happy to take credit for their own material comforts, even in a society whose very purpose has been to produce and to distribute goods, and in the process to keep the circuits of capital in constant movement. Where, at an earlier time, capitalist ideology taught that the individual was responsible for his or her own poverty, it now offers the more seductive instruction that the individual is responsible for his or her own well-being. When people were told that the sole remedy for their poverty lay within their own power, this dogma met with the greatest resistance from millions of people who knew that, however hard they worked, they could still not earn enough money to provide for themselves, their children and old people and accordingly, they repudiated the doctrine that individual effort alone can alleviate poverty. It was in this context that the great visionary alternatives of collective provision against insecurity, sickness and want was conceived; not as abstract theory, but as a living and practical response to the dereliction of all those whose lives were always shadowed by insufficiency, hunger and pain.

The changed aspect of capitalist society in our time, with its self-celebrating abundance, means that the majority of people are far less resistant to the idea that they do indeed determine their own fate. They will far more eagerly take the credit for their material well-being than they will accept being responsible for their privation, even though both are socially determined. In this way, the very tangible achievements of the capitalist system do not merely stand for what they are, but become vehicles whereby its deeper underlying ideology may be smuggled into the very heart and psyche of the people. The noble project of cherishing the individual in the West has also a darker purpose; for once individuals have taken credit for all the good things which it has showered upon them, it is only a small step to ensure that those same individuals will also take responsibility for all the socially-produced wrongs and evils that may befall them. In other words, society and social determinants are more easily eclipsed; so much so, that by 1987 Mrs Thatcher had found it possible to declare that there was no such thing as society, but 'just individuals and their families'. In other words, the very abundance of the post-war era has represented not simply one way of answering need, but has also become ideology given material form. The goods and services, the objects and purchases are not simply themselves, but also bear a heavy freight of meaning which it becomes more and more difficult to detach from them; cool, balanced judgements of gain and loss become impossible.

The more sombre side of the much advertised concern for the individual in Western society is that the same individual can be made to take personal responsibility for all socially produced wrongs as well. The system that delivers the goods is thereby separated from that which delivers the evils; and a Manichean world-view is established, in which capitalism is cleansed, innocent of all its violent and bloody scythings through the world, its cruellest visitations and exploitations, and the only flaw in the system is faulty individuals, those who stand in such shaming contrast to its shining perfection.

This means, not only that older, more familiar evils, such as poverty and unemployment, can be transformed into the failings of individuals, but all the other social and moral problems of the age can be attributed to the personal wrongdoing or deficiencies of human beings. Individualist ideology gains an easier passage into the spirit and sensibility of the people; and only makes more plausible the rejection of all collective and solidaristic endeavour. Indeed, all the misfortunes of the world can then be projected onto collective activity—the horrors of communism, the levelling doctrines of socialism, the national madness of Nazism. And indeed, just as socialist societies have erred by excess in their emphasis upon the primordial importance of the collective, so we have been mistaken in a single-minded obsession with forms of individualism that seek to deny an equally important aspect of human experience. Any society that seeks to totalize its ideology—and which society doesn't?—becomes dangerously unbalanced. Individuality is an expression of the autonomy and integrality of a human being; individualism means the unbridled celebration of it. In the West one regularly hears people say 'I believe in the individual', 'I want to be an individual', 'I want to be myself', 'I'm trying to find out who I am'. One of the great paradoxes is that the exaltation of the individual must seek its fulfilment through what are essentially mass markets: people whose individuality is actually impaired by the fact that they read the same newspapers, see the same television programmes, eat the same foods, dress in the same fashions, worship the same shadowy creatures promoted by show business. Is it any wonder that there is such a crisis of identity in so many people in the West? The ideology of individualism not only denies the social and the collective (except insofar this can be manipulated in the interests of profit), but it also denies the individual as well.

That social democracy in the West should have been caught up in the maintenance of this bizarre construct goes some way towards an explanation for its impotence and exhaustion; and indeed, hesitation before so apparently immovable a reality perhaps accounts for the reluctance of the Greens to follow through and define more precisely some of the implications of their own position. For whatever efforts are required to preserve the planet from terminal exploitation, and to bring hope to the most wretched, these are not going to be solely the work of individuals, no matter how heroic. The Green movement baulks precisely at the necessity of reformulating the collective project, the weakening and sclerosis of which has been the ruin of Labourism, and a too rigid adherence to archaic forms of which has led to the loss of plausibility of socialism.

The elevation of the individual and the disgracing of the solidaristic have led to the present political impasse. The right has made all the running, while the left has been divided, one segment hard in pursuit of the dominant right, the other segment returning to an antique fundamentalism, employing a rhetoric which has become a dead language to a majority of the people. In consequence more and more people are becoming aware of the inadequacy of existing responses to the enormities of the times. Extending and enriching those responses is the function to which the Greens, in the absence of any other plausible analysis, are called.

5 / THE MALIGNANCY OF INDIVIDUALISM

THE SOCIETY WHICH PRODUCES distortions and extremes in the name of its devotion to the individual, then conceals itself behind the excesses of individuals, disculpates itself from any part in their actions. It is as though society had dissociated itself from the infirmities and short-comings of human beings, and sought to project itself only through the pleasing aspect of its prodigious material achievements.

Occasionally, the mechanism whereby this works is revealed; usually as a result of some spectacular and monstrous crime. The sometime sleepy Berkshire town of Hungerford was the site of one such crime in the summer of 1987; a place transformed for ever by having been the setting for the first (though, alas, certainly not the last) mass serial slaying in Britain. Whenever we have looked at some of the more ugly social phenomena issuing from the United States, we in Europe have tended to shake our heads and say 'It couldn't happen here'. Sooner or later, of course, it does happen here. Britain, like every other country in the world, is a developing country, and the lineaments of that development are already deterministically inscribed in the more rugged social landscapes of the United States. We quite often use the word 'developed' to describe the countries of the West, a term that implies something static and completed. This is nonsense; it is merely an expression of our complacency, and our unwillingness to look at the direction in which we are developing; it saves us from having to confront some of the disfigurements which that form of development creates and will continue to create.

The most common reaction to the Hungerford massacre was that it was incomprehensible: 'meaningless', 'random', 'motiveless' were the words used by the press. It was a 'barbaric act', an 'evil crime', a 'stunning tragedy'. The Sun called it the 'Rambo Massacre', the Mirror 'The Day of the Maniac'. When Ryan, the murderer, was declared dead, the Mirror reported that the residents of this sedate and conservative town cheered and danced, chanting 'The bastard's dead, the bastard's dead'.

Attempts to explain seem to falter in the presence of such an enormity. Fragments of biography filtered through the media, from former schoolmates, from relatives, neighbours. He was gun-crazy. He was a loner. He had an unhappy childhood. He drifted in and out of jobs. He couldn't come to grips with life. He had always preferred guns to girls.

Yet the picture remains incomplete. Grief; disbelief; shock; but no even half-adequate account of why such things happen. None of the puzzled responses comes anywhere near to touching the causes of a day of seemingly gratuitous slaughter. In a society which provides instant explanations for everything, there was a curious and unwonted silence. Even the normally voluble experts—those sagacious representatives of a division of intellectual labour who, in aggregate, create an impression of omniscience—were awed into a mumbling mutism. 'We shall never know', they concluded.

The Prime Minister, swiftly on the scene, echoed this theme of incomprehensibility. There were, she declared, no words in the English language to describe the horror, suggesting perhaps that less delicate tongues might be at no such loss. She did give a clue, however, as to the conclusions that were inadmissible, when she stated that we were dealing with something 'unknown in this country'; for such phenomena are certainly not unknown in the United States, that source and inspiration of an enterprise culture which she is so anxious for Britain to emulate, and whose variegated and colourful products include the promotion of militaristic fantasies, cults of heroes, machismo and survivalism, a vast sex and violence industry that masquerades as provider of entertainment, a worship of fame, respect for the 'power of the gun'; and mass murders.

We had read about such things, naturally. There was the Macdonald's massacre in 1984, and we shuddered and congratulated ourselves on our more gentle, more decent way of life. The papers have always reported bewildering stories—the girl who shot her teachers because she didn't like Monday mornings, the man who murdered a hostess in a night club because she wouldn't dance with him, the lone maniac at a luncheon counter who mowed down half a dozen strangers for no other reason than that 'he didn't feel good'. It now appeared that like so many spectacular barbarisms from which we have always sought to distance ourselves, it does happen here.

The label that these things are inexplicable is actually a proscription on understanding, a taboo. We must learn to live with such eruptions of murderous violence. They are simply part of 'modern life'; and as such, a necessary accompaniment to our version of social and economic development. And nothing must be permitted to interfere with that. What must therefore remain in shadow are the social determinants in the production of crazed and aberrant individuals who, one fine day, and for no good reason, go on an orgy of shooting.

At such times it becomes apparent that the showy concern for the individual, the creed of the sovereignty of the individual is far from the whole story. The pre-eminence of the individual in this way has the powerful advantage of dissimulating society, and of absolving it from any implication in wrongs that were once ambiguously perceived as social. Such are the furthest effects of a capitalism, purified, candid and serene, with no other role in our lives than that of supreme bringer of all that is wholesome and beneficent.

Indeed, even what are still publicly described as 'social problems' are, in fact, treated as though they were solely the troubles of faulty individuals. So successful has the system been in purging itself of all its defects, that even poverty and unemployment can now, with some conviction, be presented as personal misfortunes and not as the consequence of economic and social processes. In fact, there are no longer any social and economic processes; there are just individuals. Above all, there are those individuals who are rich and successful, those we are expected to admire and to emulate, as embodiments of the highest good to which human beings may aspire.

But just as good must define itself against its opposite, so we also see, in the public discourse of newspapers and telecasts, a public procession of disgraced and fallen humanity: the rich and talented, the achievers and the generators of wealth call forth the maniac, the monster and the fiend.

Such developments are, in part, the result of the decay of political and social alternatives, the extinction of social hope; notably of the dissolution of the traditional agencies of collective resistance and struggle. Nowhere has this gone further than in the United States, which is why so many failed, denied or tormented individuals can impose themselves upon their society only by some monstrous act of terror or violence—an act that is a shadow of some equally grandiose celebration of success. It is interesting to observe that only two days before the *maniac* struck, we were invited by the popular press to contemplate the phenomenon of *Madonna-mania* that was sweeping Britain.

One of the consequences of the spreading belief that the contradictions of capitalism can no longer be resolved through political action (or perhaps it is a belief that such contradictions no longer exist, for they certainly make no appearance in mainstream political discussion) is that these must now be reconciled within the private lives of individuals. In this way, we all become the site of epic struggles, where some sense must be made of the inconsistencies of the system. Victims of injustice, those who have no outlet for their frustrations, find there is no cause, no crusade, no collective social or political activity that will address itself to their grievance. What choice do they have? How shall they express their pain to the world? Who will listen? Who cares?

If all social influences seem to have been effaced from the lives of 'free' individuals, this is merely because these have, so to speak, gone underground, become invisible. 'We used to live under capitalism', was how one old trade unionist expressed the change he had observed, 'now they tell us we live in society'. The capitalist system, in its more benign guise of market economy, has been at pains to dissociate itself from its part in any aggravation of human suffering; with such success it appears, that all that remains is the irreducible and incomprehensible alien, the maniac, the gratuitous wrecker, the gun-crazed loner. The spurned and trampled individual who can feel that he (more rarely, she) exists only through the perpetration of some ghastly action which the world must acknowledge, is only the underside of those achievements of all the heroes and stars and phantasms of perfection, those models of success we are bidden to venerate.

If we want to gain some insight into these horrors (and there is a good deal of evidence to suggest that we don't), if we want to know why there is such violence, so much emotional and psychic disturbance, why breakdown and loss of control are so common in this society (and perhaps the affluent town of Hungerford makes the location of this atrocity less random than it might at first appear), we have to look beyond the deranged individual, and track down the distortions created in him by the wider social context.

By means of its spectacular wealth, the manipulation of images and sur-faces, capitalism appears as a uniquely benign force in the world. And since there are no longer social evils, there can be only evil people. That so many people collapse under the pressure of this ideology is not surprising. Only of course, each does so in his or her *individual* way, through his or her own psychic or emotional or mental vulnerability. In this way, the socially significant forces at work are magically obscured and dispersed: above all, they remain securely hidden beneath the wrecked and mangled lives of individuals, gaining thereby camouflage and immunity. It is only when there is some grisly outbreak such as that in Hungerford that our betters rush, post-haste, not to reveal, but to shroud in unknowability that which stares us in the face. And because of what this might tell us about the nature of the society that sustains us, we would rather rest in the uneasy and precarious explanation that such things are inexplicable; uneasy, because we know that however unpredictable, the one thing that can be predicted with certainty is that they will happen again.

6 / CRUMBLING IDEOLOGIES

IDEOLOGIES THAT EXPLAIN THE WORLD (and what other purpose do they serve?) have an organic life of their own: they are conceived and elaborated, they grow and decay. As long as they can be tested against events, and they hold up with tolerable consistency, they will continue to command the faith of the people. It is only when they clearly cease to be in harmony with experience, when they are contradicted by stronger experiential evidence than anything contained in the account they give of the world, that doubts arise. Even so, the profound need of people to believe can carry ideologies over some formidable contradictions: human beings will readily be sacrificed to their truths. But once faith in their capacity for illumination and revelation begins to crumble, the process is irreversible.

This model becomes even more stable and apparently immutable when two countervailing beliefs buttress and reinforce each other, nourish and lend one another conviction by their balance and symmetrical opposition. But should both begin to falter at the same time, the crisis of faith becomes even more grave, and the dissolution of both is accelerated.

This is what we are now living through. The mutually supporting beliefs that have borne up both right and left in antagonistic equilibrium through-out at least the latter part of the industrial era, no longer appear so plausible to their former adherents, do not furnish them with the wholeness of meaning they once provided. This breakdown appears in the West in the form of decreasing political participation, a growing cynicism, a volatility in people's allegiances. In the United States, half of those eligible to vote fail to do so. The experience of more and more people appears to detach itself from the sustaining faiths which had seemed to make sense of the way things are. Gaps appear in the arguments, holes appear in the sometime

45

seamless web of explication. Dissatisfaction and hunger for more convincing and more hopeful versions of the world are perhaps what produced a spontaneous vote of fifteen per cent for the Green Party in Britain in the European elections of 1989. This can be a profoundly liberating moment, when more veracious and plausible arguments force their way through the spaces opened up. New ways of perceiving the same things occur. The traditional understanding of social and political phenomena appears inadequate; other versions of reality gain ground. At almost any point in the exhausted and sterile argument between left and right, the inadequacies of both have now become overwhelming.

Conflict between capitalism and socialism has hitherto concentrated upon the ownership of resources and the distribution of wealth; neither has questioned the prodigal exploitation of resources or the desirability of the wealth based upon it. But now that the 'externalities' of economic systems have returned to undermine them—the costs formerly passed on to the environment, and the limits upon the use of the earth's resources—arguments about ownership become subordinate to the sustainability of those economic systems themselves. This in turn raises questions about social justice: for sustainability without social justice is possible (the rich of the earth survive, while the poor perish), but social justice is impossible without sustainability (social justice, that is, to future generations, to whom we will otherwise bequeath a dead planet).

These issues insinuate themselves into all traditional arguments, subverting them as they do so. They affect discussions about society no less than about the economy; and it is only by making the connections, and by making them explicit that the Green alternative may define itself with the compelling urgency that the times demand. No doubt that alternative, too, will, in the long term, be seen to be full of contradictions; no doubt new opposing forces will show themselves. But for the moment, the Green vision remains fresh and living, not yet ossified into dogma or hardened into revelation. And in every area where right and left collude to retain familiar antagonisms in place, the Green perspective throws a stark and shrivelling light upon their dishonest pretensions, as any look at existing ideological disputes readily reveals.

In the West, social issues have been effectively sundered from the wider context. Social problems are paraded, discrete and disconnected, before a bewildered public, fragmented and impenetrable. This is perhaps the West's over-reaction to the simplistic Marxist formulation that the economic base determines everything else. It has been all too easy to flee to the opposite extreme, and deny that there is any connection between them at all. The real relationship is more subtle and more ambiguous.

Law and Order

The very clamorous devotion of the right to law and order, their noisy denunciation of crime, ought to warn us that something akin to the reverse of this is closer to the truth. If they really were so dedicated to the values they claim to uphold, it is inconceivable that there could have been an increase of one and a half million offences in England and Wales in the first eight years of Conservative government (1979-87), or that after eight years of Reagan there were 38 million recorded crimes in the United States. Is it possible that there could have been an abrupt aggravation of the wickedness of the British and American people in less than a decade? Had a far better equipped and more highly-paid police force become suddenly indifferent to its essential role in the maintenance of social order? Have we really become so powerless that we must yield to these sad developments as though they were catastrophes in nature?

There are few experiences more depressing than to hear the representatives of the traditional parties threshing around in their attempts to make sense of it all, and to keep it confined within the cramping limits of permitted discourse. In Britain, as in America, conservatives insist that it is all 'the consequence of a permissive philosophy of self-expression', the result of an alleged breakdown of discipline in the 1960s. Indeed, the British Home Secretary declared that the big increase in the number of motor vehicles has made them an invitation to more opportunistic crime (and the issue thus becomes a back-handed tribute to the economic success of the government!). The spokespersons of centre parties sagely acknowledge that there must indeed be a link between unemployment, poverty and crime, but that the relationship is not simply causal; they advocate more research, so that the connections may be precisely and clearly established. The Labour Party—that late convert to law and order, which for many years it had failed to notice was a major concern of those it still possessively refers to as its 'own people'—can respond only by speaking of the most superficial forms of deterrence: double glazing, entryphones in flats and reinforced doors, so that housebreakers may not simply kick their way into other people's houses. All parties, those providers of easy answers in every other context, are united in their agreement that there are no easy answers.

As 'debate', this brings nothing like the illumination which politicians claim: it betrays their own mystified impotence in the presence of violence and disorder. Had not the creation of wealth been promoted as the remedy for all social ills, the answer to all discontents? Well, the wealth has indeed been created, on a scale undreamed-of; and in the heart of the richest societies in the world, those that propose themselves as models to be emulated by all those declared 'underdeveloped', we find fear, violence and crime, both organized and random, to an unprecedented degree. Indeed, both wealth and crime have increased explosively, perhaps even causally. But this is a taboo, one of the many proscriptions in our apparently open society. In adverting to it, the politicians offer a public spectacle of their own ignorance and powerlessness. All that we are left with is the conclusion of a common sense that demands a hardening of the penal system, even though the prisons of the West have never been fuller. It is difficult not to feel that here, as on so many other issues, the politicians have taken an uncharacteristic vow of silence; there is a secret which those who license discussion must huddle together to conceal from public view.

For the increase in crime is nothing more than an individual response, on the part of certain sections of the poor and the excluded; those whose condition—never very comfortable—has been worsened since the Conservatives came to power as a matter of high principle, those who have neither the skills nor the opportunity to compete effectively in the market place. In other words, crime is yet another manifestation of that faith in individualism which, in other respects, is indicated as the sole path of salvation. The rise in wrongdoing is, it seems, directly related to the buoyancy of the economy, upon which the Conservatives constantly congratulate themselves. It is the very 'health' of the economy that has widened the gulf between rich and poor.

It is to this intractable reality, and not to rhetoric, that the long-term unemployed, those humiliated by make-work schemes and low pay, those on benefit, those denied and oppressed by the vacuity of their social function, must now accommodate themselves. This means that they have to come to terms, as individuals, with their exile from all those things which a majority of the people so conspicuously and lustily enjoy. It should scarcely surprise anyone if many of them come to the conclusion that they must reach out and take a share of that which has been, arbitrarily, it seems, withheld from them.

The real secret is that this individual—even if criminal—enterprise is far more acceptable to the conservatives than any political contestation of the right of the rich to have and enjoy their disproportionate share of the wealth of the affluent countries, while the poor receive less and less. In other words, there is an unspoken and secret relationship between crime (that only modest modification of forms of initiative and enterprise which the right prizes above all else) and the faltering of political alternatives, notably those of collective hopes vested in social democracy, labourism, or, more distantly, in socialism. The first element in this relationship gains the tacit assent of conservatives, while the second commands the silence of socialists. The crime figures are at the same time an indictment, both of the real social and moral values promoted by conservative versions of freedom, and of the absence of any plausible alternative that would promise more equitable distribution of the wealth that is the object of universal reverence. No wonder all discussion freezes on the smooth tongues of politicians.

The poor know that they are doomed to eke out a frugal and disgraced existence on the margins, unless they decide to determine their own fate in the only way open to them. And that means rectifying their social disadvantage and exclusion by private acts of plunder. They are well aware of the extent to which rewards are severed from effort, labour or creativity, and seem to be, not a consequence of merit, but the result of the spin of the wheel of fortune, the fall of the dice, determined by luck or chance. Seeing the killings that are made each day (in the markets rather than the streets, although they not infrequently witness those too), the fortunes, not earned but won, the windfalls, the profits and the prizes, the lucky draws and winning numbers, they can see only the flimsiest reasons for contenting themselves with the lowly position to which that same fate—or, in their case, misfortune—has assigned them.

Crime, then, is the covert and inadmissible alliance between the maintenance of the existing order (or is it a sophisticated form of disorder?) of those who are conservative in name only, sailing under the conservative banner as pirates under flags of convenience, conserving nothing but their own wealth and power. No matter who suffers, no matter what outrages and violence are committed against people—all this is a small price to pay by those who govern us, smaller by far than any living alternative that might threaten more convincing collective resistances to the inequities and iniquities of capitalism, an alternative which, in some versions of history, social democracy was to have provided.

It can be seen how crime is an inturned and diverted radicalism, a warping of popular political dissatisfactions. It represents contestatory energies confiscated by capitalism, an involuted resentment distorted by what appear to be unalterable social realities. That the conservatives can denounce crime, which exists in such benign symbiosis with their own values, and then serenely promote policies that ensure it will go on increasing, appears to prove what they have consistently proclaimed—that there is no longer any need for opposition; and as if in compliance with this prophecy, social democracy has sought to compete with the established order on its own terrain. If the conservatives can propose remedies for the very disorders they induce, they have succeeded in closing the circle: for they have reconciled what might have once been described, in a more rigorous analysis than anything offered by social democracy, the contradictions of capitalism.

Breaking up the Family

The most vociferous defenders of the family, those who declare themselves devoted to upholding its sanctity in a threatening time, are, more often than not, the very same people whose equal dedication to an extreme individualist philosophy is contributing more than anything else to the distortion and fracturing of family—as indeed, all other—relationships. It is true that in these last decades of the twentieth century, human associations and bondings have seemed perilously fragile and imperfect, ready to fly apart under the slightest pressure. And it is only natural that people should seek out the cause of such developments, lodging the blame with moral decay, the permissive 1960s, the effects of the media, or whatever.

Yet it is surely clear that the breaking of relationships is nothing more than the logical consequence of a social and economic necessity which is about the business of promoting dissatisfactions, strivings and discontents everywhere, which can be allayed (and perhaps, at the same time, exacerbated) only by the creation of more wealth. That human associations might be the first casualty of these processes seems not to have occurred to those who extol the restless and disruptive forces of capital, and then profess themselves appalled by the growing frailty and impermanence of what have always been considered the most stable and enduring of human bonds. If more and more people discover that they cannot bear to live together, if families are constantly dissolving and reconstituting themselves, if there are more teenage runaways and abused children, if the young exhibit signs of greater disturbance and stress, if one quarter of the households in Britain consist of a single person (a number expected to rise to almost one third by the turn of the century), then we are right to be troubled.

But the real violent, malevolent disrupters of human affinities, consanguinity and closeness are the forces of a relentless and invasive individualism—the proudest expression of the capitalist project in the world. If a growing number of people are finding the nuclear family a claustrophobic and oppressive place, this has nothing to do with the efforts of any wreckers or radicals (for who would they be in so conservative a time?), but is of a piece with values that promote egotism and self-aggrandisement as the most desirable motors of human endeavour. Why should it astonish anyone if tenderness and concern for each other suffer in the working out of these things in that real world whose imperatives we are always being exhorted to face? The very discontent and restlessness which the compulsion to sell more and more things to people provokes bring in their wake the most powerful dissatisfactions with each other; so that even our poor loves, our fragile cherishing of one another, with all our weaknesses, become as perishable as the commodities we use up and throw away each day. It is not possible to preach the desirability of constant innovation, of new needs, new products and fresh excitements on the one hand, and to expect permanence and stability in human affairs at the same time.

Whatever the benefits of the rich consumer societies—and these require no further celebration than that which they already receive—it is not reasonable to imagine (despite the propaganda of a busy advertising industry) that all these can be enjoyed at no greater cost than their mere monetary price. They will demand other sacrifices and penalties; and part of that price is the forfeit of rootedness and continuity, the anchoring of our affections in each other, enduring commitment. Is it surprising that those who do so well out of the existing arrangements would like to identify them with the forces of stability and certainty, when in fact, they bring in their train the cruellest disruptions, woundings and separations?

This is, of course, not new. After all, it was the growth of the manufacturing system in the first industrial era which disturbed the great networks of kinship in the countryside and brought people into new associations in the urban areas; it was economic success that created the nuclear family and saw the ruin of more extended ties of blood. The nuclear family is indeed a depleted place, where individual relationships must carry more weight than they can bear—intense emotions, jealousies, anxieties, contradictory feelings having no more expansive sphere in which to express themselves. All our lives have become more depopulated (and capitalism knows a great deal about depopulation in one form or another); we are, as individuals, simply too weak to contain such concentrations of passionate feeling.

The question has to be posed afresh. Who is advantaged by the disruption of the family, by the feminizing of poverty, by the disturbance of children in transit between other people's relationships? Who gains by the necessity of hiring carers, of buying in the attentions that loving hands no longer have time to dispense, and that fall as too much of a burden on one woman? Certainly not the human wreckage that fills the doctors' surgeries, the psychiatric wards, the waiting rooms of therapists of all kinds, and the mailbags of advice columnists.

The rhetoric of the right should never be taken at face value. The system they cherish finds the fulfilment of its purpose in unsettling and rearranging human relationships, evicting people from settled ways of living in its relentless war against the collective and the shared. The furthest consequence of these separations and sunderings would, no doubt, be a society in which no one could bear the company of anyone else for very long, so that we would all cower in our private cells, making lugubrious sorties into a menacing outside world to purchase the affection, the consolations, the sex, the comforts, the advice we require. Indeed, perhaps such a description is not so remote from the way that some of us already live.

Occasionally, the television or the newspapers pick up images of this inner desolation but they are seldom interpreted for what they are. Sometimes, we glimpse those voluntarily disappeared, the youngsters who have run away, those sad grainy pictures on the boards outside police stations, last seen wearing a blue cardigan and a summer dress; or in those television documentaries, where parents walk through the lights of Piccadilly Circus late at night, showing passers-by a photograph of their daughter in school uniform, and asking if anyone has seen a girl who looks like this.

Nor is it only the victims of families obviously broken who suffer. Who can measure the secret despair of those trying to live up to the ghostly realities of the iconography of advertising, hiding their alcoholic, their gambler, their emotional disturbance, their collective loneliness in the outer trappings of a contented conformism? They have the purchased consolations of fantasy, addictions and escape; but it is impossible not to wonder what it is *from* which they are turning their gaze, the 'average man and woman' who spend three or four hours each evening watching television.

These things are not some alien implant in 'our society', but part and parcel of its corrosive and disintegrative power over our frail solidarities. We should not be impressed if its protectors exploit an archaic rhetoric, a myth of the return, the nostalgia for a time when such cruelties were less pervasive (for other cruelties were certainly more so); we must expect them to take advantage of the sadness of those who have indeed known more sheltering and extensive family supports than anything we now see. The ability to hold together such explosive contradictions as it scythes its way through the world and through the hearts of people is the greatest tribute that could be paid to a system that has never cared how it uses up humanity in its sacred mission of separating people from their money, in selling them consolations for their own lost liberties. Indeed, by what more triumphal and uncontested means could this sublime project be realized than by sowing discord and mistrust between people? The perfect alibi is to be found in its songs of praise to the perfect commodities that it spills upon the earth with such generous and promiscuous abandon. Is it surprising that we, in our turn, should emulate its majestic progress through the world, breaking bonds, severing connections, weakening associations, until we are all cast out, unprotected, defenceless and alone against its ravages, into a society where parents can no longer be relied upon not to abuse or molest their own children, where you can trust no one any further than you can see him or her, and where the most lasting relationship is the sweet, secret and unavowed bond between the individual and what his or her money will buy?

The left also has its secrets in this area. While social democracy does not engage—except competitively—with the rhetoric of the right, many socialists exult in the breakdown of family as the destruction of the locus whereby capitalist values are propagated, even though capitalism no longer needs this archaic institution as conduit for the transmission of its messages: the air is full of them all the time. Socialists have seen in family breakdown a liberating opportunity for women, and indeed such freedoms are real; only with twenty per cent of children being raised by single parents (overwhelmingly women), it is one thing to walk out on a brutal husband, but it is quite another to be incarcerated with three children in a rundown council flat at the far end of a bus-route. The partial freedoms are always curtailed and impaired by the context in which they are doomed to operate. Many of those who see 'progress' in the wreckage of families are reacting to older forms of authoritarianism, whereby it was the family that internalized the values of industrial discipline; yet the broken and atomized families of today correspond to a transformed employment structure in which industrial discipline has had to be radically modified in the interests of training human beings as consumers as well as workers. To take pleasure in any forces that isolate and injure people in such ways as we have seen is precisely to underwrite the values of a system to which socialists once declared themselves implacably opposed.

The consequences of economic development have become disarticulated from the economic processes themselves; so that even while the latter can be seen to be functioning perfectly, the former bring into existence strange mutations and barbarities which create a split state of mind in the people. The material increase which is the object of all economic endeavour is won, increasingly, at the expense of the human needs which such increase is supposed to serve. But because of the way in which the rewards are distributed, fear of loss, the dread of a return to past poverty, the spectre of contemporary poverty all over the world, make us cling to what we know for dear life, never mind what price must be paid. Even as we pick our way across the bodies of the victims of drugs and alcohol in the streets, while we look anxiously over our shoulder for the rapist and mugger in the shadow, as we lock and bolt our doors against evil spirits that are already within, while we wonder uneasily at the poisoned and contaminated earth our children will inherit, we nevertheless still hope that nothing will come to disturb the familiar dependency, the known and customary way of living, even though this bears less and less resemblance to all the high virtues that are supposed to distinguish our civilization.

It is not enough to declare, as many in the Green movement do, that we are living in an unsustainable way, using up future resources, squandering the substance of the next generation however true this may be. People must *feel* subjectively the injustice and unsustainability of it before they will be driven to act; and that means, experience the dis-ease and dysfunction, the distress and misery caused by the way we live. For what is the abuse and disfiguring of the earth, if not the outward sign and expression of our distorted relationships with each other? It is through the internal contradictions, the lived inconsistencies, the cruelties endured by flesh and blood, the human sacrifice demanded by these rich societies that the emancipatory impulse will be engendered in people. But as long as the goods remain separated from the evils, and not judged together, in balance, we shall continue to be tormented uncomprehendingly; only when we perceive that the horrors of contemporary existence are the unavoidable attendants of all that is held out to tempt us, shall we be in a position to make a more sober assessment as to whether it is worth maintaining what is, or whether there might not be more equitable and satisfying ways of answering need, more modest and frugal demands on the earth, ways that will not be won at the expense either of the necessities of the poor or of the wasting fabric of the planet.

Our Daily Bread

The Green critique is radical and profound. It pierces the shell of all received responses and traditional practice. At the same time, it must seek to reassemble into some coherence the fragmented areas of experience into which our concerns have been dispersed, and that means reclaiming the knowledge of specialists, experts and professionals of all kinds. Those who have claimed that there is no longer any possibility of overall ideological consistency in the resistance to capitalism are looking at the decayed and moth-eaten totalizing efforts of existing socialism. But we are still in the presence of the overwhelming monoculture of money that is capitalism. The attempt of the Greens to counter this monstrosity must be both wise and rigorous.

In answering the most abstruse needs, the market economy has evolved some curious distortions in its answering of basic ones. Nowhere is this more apparent than in the realm of food and nutrition.

In the United Kingdom, 1989 was characterized by a series of scares about food: eggs, soft cheese, yoghurt, apples, drinking water, chicken and beef, and even breast-milk became the objects of greater or lesser degrees of panic. The very existence of a 'food industry', of an 'egg-processing industry' (don't our hens do that for us?), the vaunted sophistication of food technology, are a measure of the distance we have travelled in the denatured way of life which we are expected to believe represents the highest freedoms. Basic nutrition must be filtered through ever more elaborate structures in order to add value to it; not so that we may have greater choice, not to relieve our labour and save our precious time, but so that the profits of vast food conglomerates may be sustained at the level to which they have become accustomed.

If the food industry in the West looks increasingly like the chemical industry, this is paralleled by a cosmetic industry (and 'personal products' are now worth £4.5 billion a year in Britain) that is more redolent of agriculture, with its apricot balms and strawberry salves and almond shampoos and lemon soaps and elderberry body-gels. Both industries illuminate the warping of basic human needs by technological processes and forms of marketing that have become autonomous and disarticulated from their ostensible purposes—those of nourishment and cleanliness.

The food industry must, like all others, go on growing and expanding. It is clear that the market for basic nutritious foodstuffs is soon saturated: people's stomachs do not go on dilating indefinitely in order to accommodate growing mountains of food. Accordingly, the happy expedient has been found of an infinite variety of permutations in the composition of ready-made and pre-cooked recipes, as well as the addition of exotic combinations of flavours. Convenience foods, whatever advantages may accrue to the busy consumer, are even more convenient to those who reap such large rewards from laboratory-wrought nature-identical tastes and eating experiences. Sainsbury's boasts of three hundred new products a year; while the newspapers are full of gushing celebrations of the supermarket, declaring that there are up to 20,000 items to choose from in any one store.

These developments, as must be expected, have led to some curious mutations in our social life. One government minister in Britain lamented that the young 'have never learned—or have just forgotten—what their mothers took for granted in the kitchen'. It is true that there is a great popular ignorance about both the origins and content of food, notwithstanding the obsession with diet and the recent revulsion against additives and preservatives. Many teachers cite examples of children who believe that chickens come out of red-striped boxes and that fruit grows in pies, of children refusing to eat an apple when invited to pluck it from a tree. If it is true that the level of nutrition was highest in Britain when ingredients were at their plainest, in the despised and primitive 1940s, the subsequent loss of basic cooking skills must be, in large part, thanks to the effort of the food industry. Indeed, the advice offered by the government in response to the scares of 1989 astonishes by its elementary nature. It turns out that this includes washing fruit and vegetables that are eaten raw, observing 'eat-by' dates on packaged food, personal hygiene and making sure refrigerators are working properly. This can only prompt questions about what adults have been doing all their lives to have failed to master such basic information. No doubt many of us can recite the superlatives issued by those advertisers paid by the food industry, knowledge which has displaced anything taught by the schools or absorbed from parents. The level of competence at which such government advice is tendered suggests a population seriously de-skilled and disarmed in dealing with what is sometimes referred to as 'our complex society', despite the stark simplicity of its fundamental purposes. This being so, we should not be surprised if in the supreme interest of adding value to our food, it should scarcely have been noticed that the extraction of nutrients is a primary consequence. No doubt the stage will eventually be reached where we shall find more sustenance in simply eating banknotes.

All that we perceive is that as food goes on becoming more and more expensive, it is attended by an agreeable diminution in the trouble required to prepare it. This has been seen as a welcome relief to the labour of women; although there is no reason why any man should disdain a role in so central an activity as the preparation of food. But as people become increasingly dependent upon money to save time, they begin to surrender control, lose skill and power over their immediate environment. Purchasing power, in this context, becomes a substitute for other powers, abilities and capacities; it destroys know-how, wipes out memory, cripples self-reliance. It also means that re-acquisition of skills fallen into disuse costs more money—through investment in cookery classes and books, paying experts to tell us things that could so easily have been absorbed through elementary observation and imitation. I once attended a class that was run in a kitchen attached to a huge Tesco's supermarket, for the purpose of providing basic culinary information to schoolchildren and to women on low incomes; the pioneers in convenience foods evidently felt they should make amends in some small way, to those they had encouraged to forget old skills.

Thus the processing of food goes hand in hand with a curious processing of ignorance. The food writer Geoffrey Cannon declared in the *Daily Telegraph* that we have only ourselves to blame: 'If we do not take the trouble to know what is in our food, if we buy what is in the shops and eat what is on our plate thoughtlessly, we are asking for trouble. Why should manufacturers make food better than we evidently want it to be? ... We asked for salmonella because we demanded ever cheaper chicken.' This is surely untrue. Chicken became cheaper because ways were found by producers to cheapen it: competition—that holy of holies—leads to more and more bizarre practices in order to capture markets. And how difficult it is for most people to inform themselves, not only because of the equivocation and concealment of governments in their reverence for free markets, but also because of the vast resources deployed by a tireless advertising and publicity industry. Their billions are devoted, not to telling us of the dangers or drawbacks in any purchase, but on the contrary, to singing the desirability, indeed the indispensability, of everything that appears on the market. It is clear that buying and selling in the rich Western societies have become something far removed from the cosy coming together of honest providers and informed customers, but is rather a cumbersome, secretive and manipulative practice, designed principally to induce people to part with their money with the greatest efficiency. What innocent customer is in a position to know whether the pre-cooked appetising chicken supreme in the crowded supermarket has been fed with antibiotics that will conceal some diseases, lower resistance to others, or breed drug-resistant pathogenic organisms that will engender even more intractable diseases?

Here, then, we are at the heart of wealth-creation in reality. This is economic growth as it occurs, beyond the text-books of economists—the poisoning and contamination of food by feeding the remains of infected hens to other hens, and of animal carcasses afflicted with bovine spongiform encephalitis to cows. In the primordial interest of creating addictive patterns of eating, brand-loyalties, market-dependency, who can say what other nameless sicknesses, viruses, allergies, unexplained outbreaks of disease, what other kinds of expensive, laboratory-induced poisonings are being prepared for us? This is a world-wide issue, because so many big food corporations bestride the globe. Recently, in India, I came across the family of a little girl who had died, because her parents, motivated by their profound faith in the goodness of Western-style foods, had imagined that a diet of biscuits contained all the nutrients she needed to sustain her tiny life.

That so basic and easily answerable a human need as food can have become so dangerous under the sacred alchemy of the market opens disturbing questions about what other areas of our daily experience are subjected to similar distortions, whereby need is turned with such murderous consequences against life itself.

The War on the Poor

The loathing of the rich for the poor—as exemplified by the resolute policy of the governments of most rich countries in their redistribution from poor to rich—may puzzle some people, the more so since in this age of enlightenment, that hatred is far from being reciprocated. Those who have celebrated this manifestation of the decay of class conflict, instead of rejoicing at the removal of an impediment to the whole-hearted enjoyment of their wealth, have instead turned their anger on the guileless poor, in spite of the fact that these are no longer, it seems, animated by what the rich used to call the politics of envy.

The characteristic popular response to the rich today is 'lucky beggars; nice work if you can get it'. Extreme wealth excites, not the resentment of the people, but their unfeigned admiration. So how baffling it is that the rich do not return the amiable good will extended by the poor, but rather set out to punish and coerce them, to make their lives even more dreadful, by further, deliberate efforts to impoverish them.

Why should this be, when the poor ask nothing more, from a position of the greatest respect and acknowledged subordination, than to imitate their betters? No longer moved by a sour and resentful egalitarianism, they are almost without antagonism to those who are now a source of inspiration and emulation. Their masters have become, not an irritant, much less an enemy, but a model and spur to hopeful endeavour. Why do the rich and powerful appear unable to leave them to the modest preoccupations and pleasures of their station?

The eclipse of the politics of class conflict (for are we not all working class now, according to conservative politicians?) means that there is no powerful source of opposing and alternative values in the living practice of the poor, no other impulse to hopeful struggle, no other vision of how society might be more justly ordered. All the images of the better life no longer belong to visionaries and utopians, to those trying to live out another way, but are owned and controlled by the rich. What is more, they have been privatised; with the result that the poor do not represent—even rudimentarily—an alternative, but merely seek, from a position of dependency, to imitate those set above them, within the pitiful constraints of their resources.

And perhaps we may glimpse here the reason for the abiding hostility of the rich towards the poor. It may be that, after all, they copy them a little too well, mimic their ways, ape their behaviour too accurately, and throw back too clear a reflection of their manners and values, one that is far from flattering. The rich do, after all, take great pains to cloak their conduct with money, buy distance and discretion with their wealth, so that they present an appearance of the greatest urbanity and civility in all their dealings. So when the poor clearly demonstrate the primordial importance of money over morality, display the fact that no gains are ever considered ill-gotten, and that lucre has shed its pejorative epithet, that crime does pay and the best things in life cost a packet, they are not only an embarrassment, but may also cause something to stir in that redundant and vestigial organ, the conscience. In other words, the poor betray secrets, not wittingly, like untrustworthy maids and manservants disclosing salacious tales of boudoir and bedroom, but by the caricature of the mores of the wealthy which they so openly reveal. If the poor show that they can be as venal and rapacious as their masters, then it is for their indiscretion that they must be punished. Their adherence to their models has been just a little too faithful.

Into what frightening abyss do the rich peer when they observe how the poor live? Are they not, from whatever dizzying elevation, gazing into their own souls? Perhaps this is why, when they survey their own lives, they perceive there evidence of a lamentably fallen and irredeemable human nature; but when they look upon the poor, they see only criminals and malefactors, idlers, scroungers and cheats who must be castigated. Confronted by the violence, the ruined relationships, the addictions and cruelties of the bleak estates and the inner cities, the rich read there more naked versions of their own dissimulated sufferings, which they have made such efforts to conceal, in anonymous detoxification centres, private psychiatric care, discreet clinics, purchased cures and therapies, and all the attempts to heal the sicknesses of their debilitating addiction to money. Only occasionally, *their* sorrows also surface, through the newspaper scandals, the shocking court-case, the golden children destroyed by drugs, or killed while driving at 120 m.p.h. on the wrong side of the motorway, the high-class embezzling, the electronic fraud or insider dealing—things which make the nicking of a credit card or fiddling a giro or defrauding the fuel company look like the pallid and derivative imitations which they are.

Because the rich are the beneficiaries of a system which rewards them so well (in financial terms—and after all, that is the sole means whereby they define and distinguish themselves), they believe that they have an interest in concealing the human—as opposed to the mere monetary—price which they, like their poor but unacknowledged kin, also pay. The real crime of the poor is their involuntary disclosure of values and conduct and beliefs of which they are not the originators.

That the poor thus throw into sharp relief the workings of those who would shroud them in the utmost mystery, means that the wealthy will spare nothing to distance themselves from the revelations of such devotedly authentic imitators. It is a form of one-sided class warfare, in which those formerly accused of fomenting class strife have unilaterally laid down their arms. The rich are bound to dissociate themselves publicly from those whose poverty is nevertheless indispensable to them for the underlining of high moral lessons, and whom they have, god-like, created in their own image.

The decline of class consciousness, like the removal of many apparent evils, does not quite lead to the unalloyed good that might have been anticipated, for so many other kinds of consciousness appear to have decayed with it. Indeed, conscience itself seems to be one of the principal casualties. Certainly, the vision of a society without conflict in its universal deference to the otherwise curiously levelling monoculture of money has at least one fortunate by-product: it demonstrates clearly the urgent need for an alternative, something vital and energizing, once supplied by a socialism that has been recently so eager to defer to the superior wisdom and efficiency of the market economy.

This is why the new initiatives, experiments in living practical alternatives, are overwhelmingly Green in inspiration. Groups of people are trying, often against considerable odds, to pool their human resources and skills and to minimise their dependency upon material ones, to practise self-reliance and sharing, aims that might once have been identical with those of a socialism, conceived in just such hope and idealism, but slowly strangled in the snares and toils of a system whose sweet reason it has now bowed to. It may be that the Green consciousness is another metamorphosis of that which energized and gave strength to a now lost and compromised socialist vision. If Green theory remains relatively unelaborated, this is not because of any intellectual deficiency, but because the ideas are evolving out of living—and rapidly moving— experience; growing in default of more adequate interpretations of the patterns of development of both the rich and poor world. Perhaps it would be more accurate at this stage to talk of a 'Green sensibility', a way of seeing, a response to the menace to humanity and to its environment, a response that recognizes the impossibility of containing these threats within existing structures, disciplines and institutions.

We, in the West, have become so complacent in our illusion that all problems can be dealt with by modest reforms, administrative tinkering or the technological fix, that it is easy to believe that what confronts us now is no exception to past difficulties that have been successfully sur-mounted in the industrial era—the threat of a hungry and excluded work-ing class, for example, the disengagement from extensive colonial empires, the regular and recurring outbreaks of war. Yet this time, everything proc-laims the insufficiency of our reactions: indeed, despite their expressions of concern, it seems that the faith of the Bush and Thatcher administra-tions in the power of market forces is so secure that they will look to the very cause of the disorders to cure them. Indeed, if it had been the purpose of humanity on earth to lay waste the planet, its people and its treasures through the wasting disease we might call galloping consumption, no more effective instrument could have been conjured up by human imagination than the market economy. Everywhere it is allowed free passage, it leaves a trail of environmental devastation and human desolation.

7 / THE UNSUSTAINABLE CITY

WHILE INDIA REMAINS an overwhelmingly agricultural society, the proportion of people living in cities is increasing, with the result that it now has one of the largest urban populations in the world, in spite of the fact that little more than a quarter of the people are city-dwellers. In Maharashtra, in western India, people are being displaced from the countryside by pressures that include the concentration of land in the hands of bigger farmers, by the spread of cash-crops, by Western-driven 'improvements' that do away with the need for labour and depend for their success on an unsustainable use of expensive and damaging inputs.

Despite India's nominal commitment to socialism, the freest of free markets operate for those who can afford to evade the official safeguards and regulations that are overseen by a corrupt bureaucracy. The informal economy is in many ways more thriving than the formal one, even though in the years since Rajiv Gandhi has been in power, even this has tended more and more to liberalization, in imitation of Western models of development.

One consequence of this has been a sad pilgrimage of people towards urban life; a frieze of humanity uprooted and sent in search of new forms of livelihood; some in Maharashtra go to the smaller cities of Aurangabad or Nagpur. But for many more, the city means Bombay, the richest city in India. Within the next decade or so, Bombay will become one of the world's megacities; and the processes that are driving more and more former country people to seek shelter in its inhospitable shadow are being repeated in all other countries in the South.

Bombay, with its ten million people, is still a magnificent city, with its ornate buildings from the Raj, the silver dome of the Prince of Wales

64

museum, the cathedral-like intricacy of Victoria Terminus, the coloured lights of Chowpatty Beach on the perfect horseshoe of Marine Drive on land reclaimed from the sea, the old fishing communities squeezed onto the very edge of the mangrove swamps, the monumental cotton mills, modelled on those of Lancashire with their stone chimneys, battlements and ceremonial stone entrances.

Like all such cities, it is a place of the most intense energy and vitality. The efforts required each day simply to survive leave the visitor both stunned and shamed. Half the people in Bombay live in slum settlements, many of them illegal and without basic amenities. The huts have been constructed with the greatest ingenuity out of waste materials, densely packed in narrow crooked passage-ways against the pitiless sun. Yet even in these modest shelters, people are not free from harassment and anxiety—the attentions of slumlords and officials, police and *goondas*—it scarcely matters to them from which side of the law. In addition to this, they must find work in the gaps of a city economy that already looks impermeable; yet they do create work, selling, recycling rags or metal or plastic, labouring in foundries and metalworks reminiscent of Engels' descriptions of the Black Country in Britain, cart-pulling or begging, prostitution or smuggling, drug-dealing or finding a fragile stability in subcontractors to the multinationals, sewing shirts or jeans, making sportswear with pirated logos, shoe-cleaning or paper-selling. From early in the morning the city seethes with the energies of people used up in the most demeaning and exhausting activities, so that they and their children may eat.

Several hundred more migrants arrive in the city each day, driven by poverty and landlessness to seek space in the sulphurous atmosphere, on the pavements scoured by the dust so that they shine like glass. At night, people on the sidewalk wrap themselves in faded blankets, so they appear lifeless and shrouded like mummies. The congestion and pollution are stifling: there is a mere 0.25 hectares of open space for every thousand people—and that includes the traffic islands. There are three men to every two women in the city: all over the State of Maharashtra women and children wait for the remittance from the city, the homecoming of their men or the message that will tell them to join him, perhaps on nothing more than a square of beaten earth or the city pavement. People do create work for themselves at the lowest minimum for survival: however harsh city life, people rarely starve. The urgent activity looks like an inspiration to those eager proponents of an enterprise culture in the West; the vibrancy of the slums makes them, not places of despair and demoralization, but a source of hopeful and creative endeavour.

Poverty here feels different from that in the poor areas of the rich world. The desolate small towns of the southern USA, the scarred and ruinous inner cities, the bleak satellites on the edge of the conurbations in France, the boarded-up council blocks, vandalized lifts, graffiti and concrete of the estates in Britain are de-energized, empty of hope. There, people are fatalistic and impotent. The story is one of the futility of trying to do any-thing for yourself, of demoralization, of the fear of crime and random vio-lence. The betting-shop and the wired-over windows of the off-licence are the sole generators of hope. Everything speaks of the skills and abilities of people being neglected, falling into disuse for lack of any call upon them. People talk of serving a life-sentence, of their own redundancy, of wasted lives. It is the very opposite with the people of the South: there, the energies are all absorbed simply finding the money that will enable them to replace the calories spent during the day. Both represent an appal-ling squandering of the human substance. In the West, energies atrophy through lying fallow and rejected: escape into sleep, television, drink, tran-quillizers is the only balm for their spurned and wasted powers.

It is easy to see the life and eager activity of the cities of the South, with their absence of any welfare provision, as evidence that the security pro-vided by the welfare state in the rich societies of the West has undermined the independence and the creativity of the people. But you don't have to go very far before the lack of welfare in Bombay shows what happens to the poorest. The hands cupped in constant supplication for money, the mutilations of the polio and leprosy sufferers, the competitive display of deformities and wounds of accidents and untreated diseases, the people propelling themselves on a skateboard or trolley with *chappals* on their hands, the small children who can turn their very vulnerability into a busi-ness enterprise, the voices trained in cajoling humility '*Baba, Baba*', the women miming their messages of hunger outside the restaurant windows, men in rags who sit with inexhaustible patience beside the thin metal vessel waiting for the dull chink of the low-value coin—so many images of desolation seem to put a term to arguments about the value or function of welfare. There is no doubt that even those who believe the character of the people in the West has been corrupted by a feather-bedding and demoralizing system of welfare would find it disagreeable and disturbing to see re-animated in the West these scenes that are so reminiscent of Victorian London.

And yet it is true that existing patterns of welfare are ruinously expensive, and always threatening to run out of control. The trouble is that so many of the resources absorbed by welfare go for repair and maintenance (to use the mechanistic vocabulary so dear to the system) of an injured humanity which must suffer in the interests of sustaining the social and economic order—the afflictions and disorders discussed earlier. Similarly, in the cities of the South, the poor bear the costs like stigmata in their flesh: the prematurely aged bodies, the lines etched in the faces of the still young, the thin tubercular bodies, the young people stooped through carrying loads greater than their own bodyweight, the women, half-effaced through maintaining postures of constant deference, the wounds inflicted by their relentless labour bear witness to all the costs elided from the accounts of exploitative businesses, both local and transnational. What doesn't appear in the profit and loss columns scars the fragile, unique and irreplaceable individuals whose lives support these miraculous and infernal cities.

Salim lives on Apollo Bunder, the ornamental arch at the Gateway of India, erected to commemorate the visit of King George V in the 1920s. I first met him when he was eighteen, full of eager enthusiasm, despite the loss of both legs in a railway accident when he was a child. For the past seven years, he has worked shining shoes under the stone arch, surviving with the help of other vendors, hustlers and street-dwellers in the vicinity. Now twenty-five, he looks many years older. The youthful smile has gone, the face is worn, the eyes sad. The change in so short a time is shocking. If someone had taken a knife and dug it into his cheeks, they could not have damaged him more effectively than the accelerated ageing that has occurred in the insecure and predatory world which has been his home.

In the evening certain streets in Bombay are filled with the light of the smoky fires of pavement dwellers. It is as though the city were illuminated by tiny celebratory bonfires. And this is, perhaps, what they are, serving not only to cook the evening meal, but also as a kind of thanksgiving that the family has survived another day, has found the means to eat, in order to struggle again tomorrow.

On the waterfront, some children provide entertainment for the tourists; a boy of ten, and his sister, six, are displaying their acrobatic skill. He holds out his hand. She steps into it, and he raises her slowly, lifting her above his head, a tiny, dainty figure in rags. Aloft, she pirouettes, her bare foot on his bare hand; then springs with a somersault to land upright on the pavement. The small crowd applauds. A few coins fall onto the dingy piece of cloth spread on the pavement.

The street children of Bombay were brought, briefly, to the attention of the West in 1989, thanks to Mira Nair's film, *Salaam Bombay*. Their plight became, thanks to the mysterious magic of the markets, a beautiful artefact, avidly consumed. The children, however, remain on the streets, children like Prakash, now fifteen, who tells how he came to Bombay with his mother ten years ago. They were fleeing a violent husband and father in Mangalore. The mother found work as a domestic, but when she fell sick and lost her job, she simply lay on the pavement, her five-year-old son beside her, begging. After two or three weeks, she died. Prakash remained with her body for a day and night, and then left her. He lived by begging and stealing. Now he works, collecting rags and scrap leather. He still dreams of his mother, imagines he sees her sometimes in the crowds. He is haunted by what he feels is his desertion of her.

Concern for the street children is not new. Many have been working patiently on their behalf for many years. Father Plassy Fonseca has been working for Snehasadan, a charity that has monitored the lives of orphaned, abandoned and runaway children for twenty-five years. There are now fourteen homes all over Bombay. The young people come and go as they please, but they are encouraged to stay and settle in family groups of about twenty, under the supervision of house-parents, many of them former runaways themselves. Among those at present at Andheri, in North Bombay are Jagdish, a boy of nine, skeletally thin, who was covered with sores and scabies when he came to the refuge; a slightly older boy ran away after he had been mistreated by his father's second wife, scarred by the marks from cigarette burns, and still trembling from the electric shocks he had been given; a boy of thirteen who had lived on Victoria Terminus station, had been sexually abused by men, and had to be treated in hospital as a result of his injuries. The average age of those who come is twelve, but some are as young as seven or eight. Father Plassy says that over the past two decades, the type of child has changed:

> In the early sixties, Bombay was much smaller. Most children then were shoe-shine boys. They were only too pleased to be offered food and shelter. But now, institutions like ours have become unnecessary, because the children are institutionalized on the streets. They can satisfy all their basic needs there. They can find money, they can get work, they can sell drugs. Formerly, survival was more difficult. Now there is a whole street culture, 10,000 or more boys.

As the city grows, in response to the 'development' of India, so the dangers for the victims of urbanization become more intractable.

A more informal street shelter is run by Bosco Pereira at Vadala, not far from the docks. Bosco has also been working with street-children for twenty years, but he is emphatic that to treat the street-boys (and of course they are overwhelmingly male) as a problem is both unhelpful and damaging:

> The idea that he has gone off the rails and needs to be put back is a diagnosis in which he doesn't recognize himself. Institutions see it as their mission to get him off the streets, educate him. This misses the richness and the wit and intelligence of their lives. They've escaped one institution called the family, why put them into another? It's crazy. There is a myth that the children live in groups. In fact, they are intensely individualistic. There may be a functional attachment to a group—but it's instrumental, he will belong for what he can get out of the group. But they certainly don't think and act collectively.

Bosco Pereira believes there is no sense in trying to incorporate them into artificial families: this provides a false model, teaches them that their own loss or rejection of family was a deviancy.

A man in his thirties arrives at the shelter; agitated and nervous, he sits down and bursts into tears. His ten-year-old son went out to a bookstall to buy a paper, over a year ago. He never returned. The father has been all over Bombay, to the police, to the mortuary. He has come here as a last hope. He shows a creased photograph of the boy, smiling into the sunshine. This is the third parent who has come to Bosco Pereira in one week. Children simply disappear, perhaps kidnapped, sold for labour or sexual slavery. One woman whose child had disappeared from the station at Nagpur when he was eight would not leave the spot. She made her home there, making a living by making hair-ornaments of jasmine. She watched every train. After four years, she saw him alight from the Bombay express.

The children of the streets have an important function in the city's economy. For the most part, they are recyclers of waste materials. 'This must be accepted as their employment,' says Bosco Pereira. 'We ask, what are the difficulties they encounter? First, there are bullies and cheats, second, there is police harassment. Our idea is to tackle, not the boy on the street, but these other forces that prevent him from doing his work.'

The process of recycling is very complicated. The boy sells his papers, rags, glass or plastic to local buyers. He may receive fifteen to twenty rupees for a day's work. The local buyers sell to retailers and make about twenty per cent profit. These, in turn, sell to scrap merchants, again with about a twenty per cent mark-up. Then on to the wholesale dealers, those with extensive go-downs to store the material in bulk; again, the profit is about twenty per cent. Finally, these deal with the industrialists who will use the material in the production process, and may require anything from a two or three-ton minimum. Bosco has tried to form a co-operative among the boys, negotiating directly with the wholesalers, but this has proved very difficult.

> The boys don't work every day, only when they want something—a movie, drugs. At the moment they are sniffing glue, what they call 'solution'. It is carpenter's glue, used to stick *chappals*. We don't approve or disapprove. Within a few weeks of coming here, they cease sniffing. The reason for drugs is that these are a substitute for belonging. Recognition and wantedness—these are the best cure.

Food is never a problem; it is always available, from the waste-bins of the five-star hotels or airline offices. They know where free meals are to be found, the mosques and the charities that offer food to the homeless. They are 'professional eaters', eating as and when food is available rather than for hunger. Bosco Pereira does not believe in making 'cases' of the boys.

> Do you or I have a case-history? They want to forget their background, not be reminded of it all the time. People want to provide playgrounds for them—they already have the whole of Bombay for their playground. We don't teach them games with rules, because the rules will only get broken, and then the adults will be upset. When people ask what goals we have, we say none—if you don't set yourself targets, you can't be disappointed. A group of boys went back to Bangalore recently, because they wanted to see some Kannada movies. They worked to get the money. They went, and then they came back.

Mudraj, fourteen, is from Mangalore. He has a ready smile, wears ragged clothes. He ran away from home a year ago. Quite self-reliant on the streets, he is full of confidence, quite at ease. He asks questions of visitors before they can interrogate him. 'Why have you come here? What do you want? Why are you interested in us?' He tells how, a few days earlier, the boys had seen a stranger enter the compound, and go to use the lavatory. They had been told to report any intruders, so they slammed the door on him and locked him inside. He turned out to be a CID detective. When they knew they had a cop locked in the lavatory, they were overjoyed. He banged and shouted and threatened. They said 'This is the man who puts us away for months or years without even thinking about it. See how he feels after just five minutes of his own treatment.'

During the past seven years, it is observable that the promise by the ruling Shiv Sena Party—extreme Hindu communalist—that it would clear the city of pavement dwellers has, to some extent been realized. Certain areas where there were rough shelters of tarpaulin, polythene and hessian have been 'beautified'; gardens have appeared with the names of sponsoring companies sprouting amid the flowers—Godrej or Balsara or Mafatlal. But the people who have been displaced have not gone away. They are simply less visible in the affluent area than they once were.

Almost every week, somewhere, huts are broken, the building materials confiscated by the authorities. More often than not, the people return the same evening to rebuild ruined homes and lives. One street in Ghatkopar, off the Lal Bahadur Shastri Road, has been razed at least once a year. In 1988, this occurred in June, just before the rains. Without warning, the bulldozers arrived: it is nearly always at eleven in the morning, when most of the men are at work, and only women and children are left to defend their shelters.

The huts were built against the stone wall of the BEST (Bombay electricity company) compound—the brick-built apartments for municipal workers. The people used to construct their homes with wood and metal, but now that demolitions are so frequent, they use flimsier materials—bamboo and sacking. The people cannot go away. They have nowhere to flee to, and in any case, their supply of work is close by in the industrial estate.

Early in 1989, many families were working at mountains of blue and pink scrap paper, off-cuts from a printing works. The workers must separate the paper from strips of cardboard, and fill hessian sacks with it. They are paid thirty paise a kilo. Although an individual earns no more than ten rupees a day, a reasonable income may be attained if several members of the family work together. Some of these are young children, no more than five or six. The people do not deal directly with the company that produces the waste. It is channelled through a middle-man, who gives out work to those he favours. The works-owner would never be able to exercise the same control over the workers as this man, who knows how much he can expect from each family, and can make sure they don't sell it elsewhere at a higher price.

Many of the women here work as domestic servants. A girl of fifteen, nimble and energetic, may clean three or four houses, and earn 300 rupees a month; while Aisha, a woman in her late sixties, earns only sixty rupees a month, working in two houses. An elderly man from Uttar Pradesh, sorting paper with the help of his small grandchildren, says 'What can we do? The only other choice for poor people is to steal. And it's only the rich who can run fast enough to escape the police.'

In one hut, where the threadbare canvas scarcely attenuates the heat of the sun, a mother and daughter are working. Two small children are eating plain rice from a blackened tin pot. The woman's husband has run away and left them with no means of support but the work they can do on the waste paper, and that may all be finished within a few days. Now, says the younger woman, her mother has arrived from Hyderabad, where she was staying with one of her sons, who treated her badly. He said she was too old to earn, but not too old to eat. In these communities, where there is such a dramatic surplus of men over women, there is always the possibility for women to turn to prostitution for money.

A family of leather-workers are squatting under a rough canopy. They too have recently been evicted from a hut for which they paid 10,000 rupees, broken for the sake of a road-building scheme. The man is mending a pair of boots. They belong, he says, to a policeman; he must repair them so that their owner may come and kick him and his children with them.

Govinda is twenty-one. The sole support of his family, his father is infirm and can no longer work. His mother stays at home to look after her husband and two younger children. Govinda works three hours a day as a clerical assistant for 300 rupees a month. In addition, he gives private lessons in maths and English. He wants to become a teacher. He goes to college in the evenings to study for his degree, paying 150 rupees a month in tuition fees. A sensitive young man, he writes poetry in English. All his energies are directed towards self-improvement. He cannot think of marrying yet; in consequence all the feelings and desires of early adult life go into his poems that are full of suppressed erotic longing.

> Where there is a great love
> There is a Miracle.
> Some say love is the lake of sorrow
> Others say love is an ocean of tears.
> Others are in fear, some are sincere,
> Some say love is a vale of death,
> Others say love is end of life
> Like the edge of a knife.
> The body dies
> But the soul is alive.
> Where there is a great love, there is a Miracle.

Behind the stories of migration and upheaval that drove so many of the people to live here, is a recurring pattern of change in the village and the countryside. You hear, again and again, of debt and landlessness, the inability to sustain farming because of the impossibility of affording the expensive inputs, because of the division of land between family members, of having to buy water now that the water-table has fallen so low in some districts. It is a picture of 'development' that doesn't have its origins, but merely its consequences, in these slum settlements, which are nevertheless so full of energy. Few people say they came to Bombay because of the bright lights or the lure of an easy life: for most people, it is a story of the most desperate necessity, and of a sorrowing and only provisional leave-taking of the familiar home-place, and the consoling dream of the return.

It is possible to celebrate the spirit of the people, and at the same time, condemn the conditions in which that spirit must endure. One little boy, found abandoned after the riots in Bhiwande in 1983, was taken in by a family here. A very able and intelligent child, he made great progress at school. The family's own children became jealous of him, with the result that he was turned out onto the streets to fend for himself. He survives by collecting metal dust and swarf from the industrial estate. The schooling of the children of a former construction worker had been similarly interrupted. Their father had been beaten by a foreman on a building site; he fell and hit his head, damaging the brain. Now looked after by his wife, he is unable to do anything for himself. The three children must all contribute to the family budget, and although they go to school in the evening, they are often so tired from their factory labour that they fall asleep over their books.

At the corner of the street are some low shacks of crude construction, barely one metre high, so rudimentary that the people can scarcely sit upright in them. These belong to migrant workers from Karnataka, who come to Bombay every year in the dry season. They are stone-workers: they buy stones that are rejected by the big construction firms, and out of these fashion mortars and pestles. Half a dozen men and women sit, rhythmically chipping away at granite boulders with chisel and hammer, shaping the round bowl and smooth pounder, tapping a dull stone music in the hot afternoon glare. The finished articles are sold for twenty-five to thirty rupees; it is only the seasonal migration to Bombay that earns them enough to avoid borrowing from moneylenders before the next grudging harvest on their poor land.

A well-dressed couple are touring the area: they introduce themselves as social workers. They live, it appears, in the new flats that gleam, white, in the sun, soaring over the dusty hutments of the poor. The man says he works for *Reader's Digest*. The word 'social worker' turns out to have a very elastic meaning. They actually represent the rich people in the new apartments, and have appointed themselves to keep the poor in their place, exhorting them to encroach no further up the hill and to keep the few roadside plants well-watered. Social workers, exercising their function on behalf of the privileged, represent an aspect of the division of city labour which I had never before encountered.

The destroyers of the homes of the poor don't always have it all their own way. In the High Court, amid the waving palms and the Gothic Raj architecture, in early 1989, a petition is being heard from the women of Sophia Zuber Street, near Bombay Central, for the return of their household possessions, illegally confiscated when their houses were demolished in November 1988. Court Number Six is an austere room, with tiled floor, wooden benches, whirring fans stirring the papers on the desks. There are bookshelves from floor to ceiling, with leather-bound works on jurisprudence, metal lockers, white strip-lighting, and lecterns for the lawyers. The judge is a woman, as is the lawyer representing the evicted people. The judge sits on a raised dais, and after every intervention, she dictates the proceedings to a man sitting at a right angle to her in front of a battered typewriter. The lawyers address the judge as 'My Lady'. The proceedings are in English, which means that the women who have brought the petition cannot understand. They remain, however, patient and attentive, watching the examination of the Chief Officer of Ward Six, the man responsible for the removal of the bedrolls, vessels and clothing. Certainly, their possessions never amounted to much, but they represent the necessities of life to those on the pavements. The women look incongruous in their olive, dark crimson and yellow sarees; they are accompanied by some of the women from SPARC (an organization working for the rights of women pavement-dwellers), who have been pioneers in defending the rights of people living on the streets of Bombay.

Mr Ghone, the Chief Officer, is dressed in a khaki suit, a neat man about forty, plump and apparently unruffled by the fuss that is being made. He alleges that the huts were cleared because there had been a fatal road accident at the spot involving a child. The municipality plans to erect railings to protect schoolchildren. Mr Ghone denies that any belongings were taken, simply the materials of construction, in accordance with the law. He does not remember any request for the return of the belongings. He always issues instructions that people's personal effects should not be touched during demolitions. If there had been any complaint, it would have reached him, because only unusual requests are referred to him. A letter is produced from the women of SPARC, complaining about the theft of household goods: 'No, this has never happened before.' Did he recall seeing the letter? 'No.' And yet he would remember unusual complaints? 'This wasn't unusual.' So they routinely steal people's goods? 'I don't remember.' He is clearly confounded by the vigorous woman lawyer, and the judge is clearly impatient with his selective amnesia.

Afterwards, the women of Sophia Zuber Street are jubilant. They had given testimony earlier, lucid and precise in their memory of who took what, who dropped a child onto the ground, who kicked the little boy trying to protect the home. All four women present are domestic workers. Kamru Nissa, Banoo, Zohra and Zamida all work in flats close to where they live, cleaning, washing, cooking. They leave the court in time to go to their places of work. The beneficiaries of their cheap labour raised no protests over the destruction of their huts, even though if the women are compelled to move, they will also forfeit the advantages of employing them.

It took until May 1989 for the legal judgement to be delivered. In it, Justice Sujata Manohar held Bombay Municipal Corporation and its officers guilty of contempt of court.

In the proceedings taken out by two women pavement-dwellers on their own behalf and on behalf of nineteen other pavement dwellers residing on Sophia Zuber Road, Justice Manohar, whilst passing strictures against the Bombay Municipal Corporation, ordered the Corporation to pay to the pavement dwellers 10,090 rupees in full recompense for the belongings unlawfully seized during the course of the demolition.

On the Northern edge of the city is Dindoshi, not far from Film City, where some of the pavement dwellers from Bombay Central were relocated two years ago. It is a rocky, stony site, with no amenities. The land was not granted them by the Corporation as of right. They must pay rent, which the municipality calls 'compensation', for the permission to occupy this land on a temporary basis. This 'compensation' has been set at forty-seven rupees a month, and backdated to March 1987, when the people first came, 'Dumped' as they say, 'like rubbish picked off the pavements of Tardev and Byculla'. Such large sums are impossible for people who depend upon a daily wage at survival rates. One consequence is that many who came here have already left, and gone back to occupy other pavements, near Mahalaxmi Racecourse and Bombay Central station. Others take the bus and train to continue the work they were doing earlier— selling fish, domestic work, factory labour, drink, fruit and snack stalls, cleaning and cooking in big hotels.

Some have illegally sold their piece of land and the hut they built to people with money, who can afford to erect a more solid structure or open a shop; with the result that even this basic housing for the poor is being pressurized by those who have the economic power to buy them out. The only resistance has come from a group of women, the Mahila Milan, organized by SPARC, who have started a co-operative, which is trying to buy a piece of land here for thirty families. They are negotiating with the municipality for a low-lying and barren parcel of ground; only by owning the land will the poor ever gain control over their own lives. One woman, whose husband works for the municipality, said:

> There is no resettlement policy for slum and pavement dwellers. Local officials take advantage, they sell documents to people like *channa* on the road. People from outside, *goondas* and slumlords, move in, and they frighten us into selling our plots. Those who had no money to build a house here handed their documents over to smugglers, builders, doctors, Marwaris. Fifty per cent moved out in the first months, now seventy per cent of those who came here from the pavements have gone.

As long as the poor lack security of ownership, they will always be ousted by those who are economically more powerful. Although the co-operative is demanding the purchase of land, they would settle for a long-term lease. There are now three thousand families at Dindoshi. Three years ago, it was uninhabited, in the shadow of a fenced-off wild park and of the grandiose structure of the Indira Gandhi Research Centre. Now it has turned into yet another slum, with a population of about twenty thousand. The poor call the municipality *Ulti-palti*, which in Hindi suggests confusion and the word meaning 'sick'. The story of the people here is of absence of facilities and deteriorating conditions of life; at least where they used to live, though on the pavement, was close to the sites of their labour. Here, there is no work. One young man was working in a unit making photographic albums for eight rupees a day, less than half the minimum wage. A woman, originally from Lucknow, broke her leg on the stony ground and could not work at all for five months. She say snakes come out of the rocks and get into the houses. 'You look out of your door and expect to see tigers leaping over the stones.' One young woman from Tamil Nadu is expecting her first baby. Her husband works for the municipality, and they have built a sizeable hut; inside there is a bed, some tin chairs, a shrine to Ganesh; over the door, a cluster of green chillies and a lime. Although her husband earns 1,000 rupees a month, they had to take a loan of 13,000 rupees to build, at a rate of interest of ten per cent a month. On a piece of ground adjacent to the house, she has made a cool garden; sadapoli, henna-plant, medicinal herbs for sprains and headaches. A small palm and a creeper form a canopy, providing a little shade from the sun.

> It is worse here than living on the pavement. There is no work. We have to take loans and get into debt. There is no school after the seventh standard, you have to pay to send your children to private schools. There are seventeen doctors in the slum, of varying degrees of competence and fraudulence. We have to queue for kerosene because there is no electricity. The water is erratic; often turned off for hours at a time.

With growing dependency on money in this remote barren place, they have truly entered upon the life of the city. The market economy has them locked in tightening embrace, from which they will never again be free.

On a second site at Dindoshi, three hundred and ten families have been relocated from Colaba, the wealthy area near the Taj Hotel and Gateway of India. They had settled originally on a piece of waste ground, but were removed in the interests of 'beautifying' the city. They had chosen to live in Colaba because it was close to where they worked—domestic workers, cart-pullers, construction workers, fish-processing workers, vegetable sellers. Again, there is no work in their new location, so they must add the costs of one and a half hours travel each way, even though the jobs were already low-paid, barely enough to maintain their families.

The huts have been built on the bare rocky place which was formerly a quarry. The terrain remains uneven, with ragged red boulders exposed, and is bounded by cliffs of stone, on which other communities have built their houses. Raj Kumar travels each day to Nariman Point in Colaba, where he has a juice-stall. In spite of the need to pay one of the street-boys to keep an eye on his stall at night, it is still worth his while to keep up the business, because that is a tourist area; and in the evenings, the seafront is full of elderly Parsees taking the air, and providing him with his living. Vijay was working for the municipality; his hut was destroyed by his own employer. Muni works as a domestic at four different houses in Colaba: she leaves home at five in the morning, and returns home at seven p.m. She earns 500 rupees a month, but must pay thirty-five rupees for transport—bus and train. One man works as a cleaner at the German Consulate, another is a tailor; a boy of sixteen sells samosas at Hutatma Chowk: yet another sells lemon, lime and orange juice from a cart near the Gateway of India— he doesn't need a licence, but has to pay the police to be left alone. An elderly man works at the Oberoi Towers Hotel, cleaning the stone floors and the curtains in the foyer. Many others are casual labourers, construction workers, some paid by the day—twenty, twenty-five rupees. They are part of a vast army of servitude, self-effacing, invisible to those whose lives are graced with the amenities they furnish; what is it to the rich if they must spend four hours a day in crowded trains and buses, as long as they are on hand with the cool drink, the meal appears out of thin air when it is required, or the service they offer is available on demand.

The most coveted jobs are with the big companies. One man working for Hoechst India is paid 1,200 rupees a month; another, with Cadbury Schweppes, 1,400 rupees. It is an irony which doubtless does not concern the transnationals, that their workers should live in rough, squalid houses, besides which the factories in which they labour are like palaces. The products appear in the shops, neatly sealed in clean packages; and it is almost as though the workers were trying to live up to the prestigious objects they produce, since they emerge from even the most pathetic hutment in clean shirts and neatly pressed trousers and immaculate sarees.

Mrs Shende is a widow. Her husband died seven years ago, and she has raised her son and daughter alone. Bagapa is seventeen; he is still at school and his mother hopes he will get a job in government service. The family came from near Madras when the sole earner in the family died. Mrs Shende goes to Colaba to clean and cook. She must be up by four-thirty each morning, and works seven days a week, with just a week's holiday. She is doing it, she says, so that her children won't have to work as invisible hands in other people's houses all their life. Bagapa is well aware of his mother's sacrifice; to show it, he has constructed an elaborate garden in front of the hut, a canopy of green among the stones and rocks. It is protected by wire against scavenging animals, and covered with morning glory, the blue trumpets in full flower over the heart-shaped leaves; there is karela, bitter gourd, and beds of marigolds, tulsi and cascades of green creeper. There are rusty Palmolein tins with herbs and plants which they have brought back from Tamil Nadu. The boy takes great pride in his art, which expresses the family's memories of their rural origins, the poverty and the sadness that drove them all this way in the search for economic survival.

When I next saw Bagapa, some months later, the garden was still immaculate, but he had been compelled to leave school. He was working on a building site; already his arms had grown muscular and his hands calloused from the work. The idea of working in government service had been forgotten.

This community became close-knit and defensive while the people remained in Colaba, but that cohesion has been weakened now, with the distance from work and the amount of time required to get there. Indeed, some people have abandoned their huts, and have gone back to live close to the workplace—some sleep on the pavement or share the house of relatives. This means that there are a number of empty places, some of which have been occupied by squatters who were not part of the original community, by prostitutes and smugglers. One hot day in March 1988, the men took a day off work (and that means real hardship to those who earn only enough to live from day to day), to break the nine huts which they had identified as being used by outsiders. The operation is conducted in almost military style. Armed with hammers and bamboo staves, twenty or thirty men, with red armbands, prepare to demolish the buildings. There is an air of great excitement and anticipation; crowds of children gather as the group marches off purposefully. They fall to, prising apart the frail but surprisingly sturdy structures. Clouds of dust rise from the hessian, particles of rust from the fraying metal fill the air. The bamboo frames are torn apart and dismantled. The men work with some relish. They know all about breaking huts—it has been done to them so many times. The houses fall in a collapsed heap of polythene, rattan and sacking. A film of dust settles over everything, altering the colour of people's arms, faces, clothing. In some huts, a few belongings are rescued from the wreckage— a bedroll, some cooking vessels, some clothes.

In one of the houses to be demolished, a middle-aged woman is waiting. She claims the hut is hers. The men pause in their work. Does anybody know her? She says she was here even before the pavement dwellers who came from Colaba; she has more right than any of them to be here. Nobody knows her. She is simply laying claim to a house that someone else built. Who knows what she wants to use it for? She may be a prostitute. They proceed with the destruction of her shelter. She tries to prevent it, holding them by the arms, imploring. They shake her off. They say that no outsiders can be admitted to the site. Last week, a blind man had begged them to let him live here; to have done so would be to start a rush of people claiming shelter. The people here have been officially recognized as having the right to stay; if the community becomes diluted with strangers, they may all be moved on again.

In the beginning, the mood had been good-humoured; later, something of the negative power of community made itself felt—its rejection of those who do not conform. The party makes its way to the edge of the slum, near the main road. There, they knock at the door of a substantial hut, where a young woman lives with her mother and two young children. The place is owned by her brother, but he is away studying. It appears that she has been inviting men into the house and charging them money for sex. What makes it more complicated is that she comes from Aurangabad, which is in Maharashtra, and the men she has been entertaining are members of Shiv Sena, the extreme Hindu communalist party which governs Bombay. They are against migrants who come to Bombay from outside of the state of which Bombay is the capital. One of their slogans has been Bombay (or Mumbai, in Marathi) for the Maharashtrians. Shiv Sena are also anti-Muslim, and by their fundamentalist religious views, they are also a threat to the *Dalits*, the Untouchables, and the scheduled tribes and castes, the poor and oppressed, to whose uplift the secular government of India has always been committed. Much of the strength of Shiv Sena is in the slum areas, but not where the majority of people come from outside the state, as is the case here. Last week, fifteen Shiv Sena supporters had turned up; there was a fight, and several people had been injured. 'If it happens again, there will be murder.'

The men gather round the hut. The woman's mother, old and bent and pathetically thin, weeps and denies that her daughter is a prostitute. The younger woman shouts her denials defiantly, but she is trembling, and her hands are shaking. A group of small children are marshalled around the hut, and are asked to describe what they have seen while playing in the vicinity. The men encourage them to chant their disapproval of the woman. She will have to leave. See, our children know what is going on. They single out one little girl of about five, and question her. What have you seen? Have strangers been here? What kind of strangers? The child is bemused and does not answer. The old woman calls the little girl to her, and puts an arm round her. She is our friend. There is a long argument. The woman's two children cry and cling to their mother's saree. She offers to move to another part of the slum. No, they must go. They decide, however, not to demolish the hut. If the woman gets a job, proper work, they can come back.

The disciplinary role of community could not be more evident. The constant threat from outside has made it introspective and suspicious. While the constant fear of demolition and loss of livelihood is present, there is little space to allow individuals scope for self-determination and the opportunity to be different.

The resistance to Western-inspired models of development is by no means confined to the efforts of the dispossessed to fight for basic needs instead of economic growth. Perhaps some of the Greens' greatest allies are to be found among those who are seeking to keep faith with that other, eclipsed model that is indigenous to India and outlined by Mahatma Gandhi.

Sacred Cows and Bullshit

India's politicians frequently invoke the spirit of Gandhi, but the living hopes he embodied have long been by-passed, preserved only in the embalming fluid of official piety. The integration of India into the world economy continues; collaborative ventures with Western companies make India an ideal dumping-ground for obsolete technologies, tethering the country more closely to the Western pattern, while older practices of self-reliance and sustainability are eroded. The market economy everywhere displaces traditions of more modest resource-use.

A *satyagraha* (non-violent protest) against such forms of development has been pursued by Gandhians for the past seven years, focused upon the vast slaughterhouse at Deonar, in the heart of industrial Bombay. A constant vigil has been maintained at the abattoir, where 11,000 animals are killed daily, including 7,000 bullocks, cows and buffaloes. It is a place of appalling noise, blood and filth. The animals pass through jets of cool water, then hot water; they are stunned and slaughtered, and the skins removed as they are dying. The hides then go to the slum area of Dharavi—Asia's largest slum—where the remains of the flesh are scraped off, the skins are treated and tanned, ready for export.

Gandhians from all over India have been coming to Deonar since January 1982. They are routinely arrested every day, both here and at the air cargo terminal, from where meat and hides go to the Gulf, Europe and the United States. Their action is no longer reported by the media, and in any case, their intentions have been systematically misrepresented: the Hindu fundamentalists have manipulated their argument to their own communalist advantage, while others have accused the *satyagrahis* of religious obscurantism ('cow-worship'), of a vain resistance to 'progress' (by which they mean India's urgent need of foreign exchange, with which to import luxuries for the élite).

This is a travesty of the purposes of those who are animated by a pass-ionate belief in self-reliance, and village-based production for need. Achyut Deshpande is seventy-one, a soft-spoken veteran of the independ-ence struggle. He worked with Gandhi, and later, with Vinoba Bhave in the *bhoodan* (land-gift) movement, when he walked through India, urging the rich to share some of their land with the poor. He was jailed nine times by the British, and spent seven years in prison in the 1930s, for agitating against the Nizam of Hyderabad, then a feudal lord.

Achyut Deshpande and his fellow-protesters occupy the top floor of Sarvodaya Hospital at Ghatkopar, a secluded compound, with a huge pink-painted lotus-flower in the couryard, and acacia trees sheltering it against the noise and pollution of Lal Bahadur Shastri Marg. It was a former TB hospital, but with many TB patients now treated at home, the *satyagrahis* can occupy disused wards. This month, the people have come from West Bengal and Uttar Pradesh. The walls of the ward are peeling, the fans broken. The protesters sleep on battered metal cots, with minimal possessions—a bedroll and cover, a tin box, some clothes strung out to dry. There is a picture of Gandhi on the wall, garlanded with fresh marigolds:

> Bullocks are the instruments of labour of the eighty per cent of Indians who live by agriculture—the very basis of the village eco-nomy. The constitution of India states explicitly that as generators of rural income, bullocks and cows may not be slaughtered, although bullocks over fifteen years old can be killed in some states. But the market for meat and skins requires the carcasses of much younger beasts. Obviously, if they die of old age, they are not edible. The law is there, but this trade in cattle is flouting the law. What we say is, either abide by the law of the country, or abolish the law.

When bullocks are sold on the free market, the price rises and the poor can no longer buy—indeed, they are tempted to sell their own cattle. 'How can the peasant compete with the butcher who comes with handfuls of petro-dollars in search of meat?' A law was enacted in India in 1937, that if someone defaults on a loan from a moneylender, the lender is entitled to take the clothes, possessions and grain of the debtor. But he may not touch the utensils, the instruments of labour, neither land nor bullocks.

This means that the butcher now has greater power over the people even than the moneylender.

There are other malign consequences of the export of cattle from villages. The organic manure is lost, the bones of dead beasts no longer enrich the soil. This further opens the way to the necessity for high-cost inputs of fertilizer. The growing dependency on chemical fertilizer in the long run becomes prohibitive and exhausts the land.

> More people are being forced to sell their land, and they come to live in the slums of Bombay, Madras or Calcutta. If we continue in this way, then even the boast that India is self-sufficient in food—it's a strange sort of success anyway, when forty per cent of the people cannot afford to buy enough to eat—will sound even more hollow than it does today. Artificial fertilizers are to the land what an injection is to the body—a drug.

The present campaign is, above all, about economics and social justice.

> Westerners say 'Oh, Hindus worship the cow'. It is true that the cow has been elevated above other beasts in the ancient scriptures. But in those countries where the horse is yoked to the plough, the killing of horses is taboo. Their god ordered Muslims not to slaughter horses. It is the economic function of the animal that leads to its being venerated, not the other way round. If the horse had been the principal instrument of agricultural activity in India, it would have been sacralized. A good thing told by any religion remains a good thing. In the same way, the calendar for sowing crops is recorded in the *Vedas*—you sow wheat in one month, pulses in another; if you depart from that calendar, you get no crop. That doesn't make it a Hindu law.

The *satyagrahis* believe that the government of India is guilty of fraud, and suicidal fraud at that, by allowing the economy to pass into the same pattern as that of the West, which has come to such a crisis of sustainability. The forces of violence work in two ways—through physical coercion and through economic exploitation. 'We are not members of any political opposition. As peacemakers, we do not vote. But if a government is the enemy of its own people, where shall the people seek redress?'

Mr Deshpande says that when people were struggling against the British, their reasons for coming together were submerged in the basic fight. There were among them followers of Gandhi, politicians who wanted home rule for their own ends, traders who thought they would get rich, others who just wanted an adventure in life. After Independence, the cement that had bonded them was no longer there, and they went their separate ways:

> Gandhians have always been in a minority. But now that India is governed by malign international forces, freedom has to be fought for all over again. In the villages, all that the people want is peace and a secure sufficiency. This pollution of greed and money will pass away. Struggles for liberation are never won, but must always be renewed; not with hate, but with peace and persuasion. Gandhi was no accident. He was a flower of the culture, also influenced by Western liberalism. A great man is created by his age, and is the creator of the next. Gandhi's thought was marked by Ruskin, Tolstoy, Thoreau. *'Sarvodaya'* is Gandhi's translation of Ruskin's *Unto This Last*; *Daya* means 'uplift' in Sanskrit, 'uplift of all'.

Vijay Kumar Anand is one of a new generation of Gandhians taking part in the *satyagraha*. A passionately determined man of twenty-five, he has been to Bombay fifteen times since the protest began. From Mirzapur in Uttar Pradesh, he is a bookseller.

> Of course, some farmers will say that old cattle are useless. But they can be used properly. The manure can go into a gobargas plant, the urine is a natural fertilizer, the hides can be used by local artisans. People say that old cattle just eat up precious grass; but that is because many farmers sell the grass that grows locally—like everything else, it goes from the village towards the markets, undermining the local economy. Everything conspires to export the fertility of the soil. In the same way, oilseeds used to be pressed in village *ghanis* and distributed in the neighbourhood; now oilseeds go to Bombay or wherever, to be processed in commercial mills, and are then brought back to the villages for sale at a far higher price. Village industries were destroyed by the British, and governments of the past forty years have continued this same process.

Aparesh Das is thirty-four, and from Calcutta. He points out that in the recent drought, many cattle died. The survivors therefore become more precious. This has no doubt occurred throughout history, leading to the heightened value of cows. 'What we see is the making sacred of useful things. Take the pipal tree. It grows in rocky arid places, where few other things grow. It provides shelter against the sun. The fruits attract birds, and these, in turn, bring the seeds of other plants. This can regenerate barren areas; no wonder the pipal tree is sacred.' This is probably why money has become the object of such veneration in the West—the means of exchange have been falsely identified as the source of survival itself.

The Gandhians at Sarvodaya Hospital are anxious for their struggle to be seen for what it is, not as some archaic religious obsession, but at the heart of resistance against the forces that are dispossessing the poor of the means of their livelihood. In their concern with social justice, sustainable development and balance with the natural world, they see the Green movement in the West as their natural ally. 'Gandhi was inspired by the West as well as by traditional Indian culture. Similarly, people like Schumacher were inspired by Gandhi. None of us owns the truth; there is, after all, only one planet, and we must all live together on it.'

The existing shape of development in nearly all countries of the Third World is an imposition upon indigenous traditions that have been disgraced and eclipsed by the glamour of Western technology. These exogenous forces have disrupted tradition and customs, broken sustainable practice, in order to open up so-called sovereign countries to the deterministic path that originates in the West. At the same time, great violence is done to the people, re-forming the psyche and sensibility of those who must be brought to see all that emanates from the West as emancipation; and this is another of the protean and sometimes subtle forms of colonialism.

Memories of Underdevelopment

The old woman sits upright on the veranda of her bungalow, away from the glare of the sun, crocheting a pink table-mat. She is ninety-three, upright, proud and dignified. Behind her, solid Victorian furniture, a carved screen with frosted panels, an ornate brown leather sofa. The fan whines softly as it keeps the humid air in movement. The peaceful scene could scarcely be further from that evoked by her memories, the hardship, the arrogance and racialism of colonial officials, and even worse than that, the frequent visitations of plague.

> When the plague was coming, we always knew, because the rats would come and die at our feet in the houses. Then people fled into the fields. They would build a rough shelter, stay there until the rats no longer died. In some families, there were three deaths a week. The gravediggers dug only a shallow trench, barely covering the bodies. My own mother and father died when I was ten. I was looked after by Belgian nuns, and then apprenticed to a dressmaker. Later, I taught at the school.

Her son says,

> The people knew that the plague was spread by rats. Only the authorities were persuaded to do nothing about it by a doctor working in Bombay, who was experimenting with a vaccine, and wanted to test it. It was already known that improved sanitation was the most effective measure. Plague had been eradicated in Cairo by improving the drainage system. But here in Bombay, it was allowed to continue for the sake of the work on the vaccine. There were waves of plague into the 1920s.

As a child, the old woman spoke Portuguese. Despite the fact that Bombay was given to Charles II as part of the dowry of Catherine of Braganza, the Portuguese had already christianized the people on this part of the coast with that violent and ineffaceable effectiveness that characterized their rule. Indeed, the old villages, enclosed now by busy roads and markets, still retain the aspect of Mediterranean towns, with their crooked streets, shingled houses, carved wooden stairways and verandas and cream-washed stone. There are crosses erected in gratitude wherever people survived the plague; 'Antonio Gonsalves, 1824'. Some bear inscriptions: 'What is hateful to you, do unto no man.'

The people of Bandra—once known as the Queen of the Suburbs, but long absorbed by the relentless embrace of India's second largest city— still call themselves 'East Indians', perpetuating thereby the name of the Company on this westernmost coast of the Arabian Sea. They form a particularly close-knit group, distinguished by their piety and an archaic civility of manner. Their psyche, their very spirit, have been the sites of shadowy dramas for possession by colonial powers. The triumph of the British over Portuguese culture shaped them into a local gentry, an educated stratum who were to become the inheritors at the time of independence. Many now see themselves as defenders against more recent forms of colonial invasion and domination, the values associated with a new transnational wealth, symbolized for them by Sindhis and Gujaratis with their showy modernistic apartments, imported cars and intercontinental travel. Yet others seek liberation from this perpetuation of what they feel are alien conflicts, and seek to reclaim ancient identities from beneath the layers of imposed cultures and borrowed values, where not even their names were authentic, their faith was that of their conquerors and their language not their own.

If the new rich are somewhat despised by the old Bandra families, this is perhaps because they were looked down upon by the British administrators, military families, collectors and railway officials who lived in ornate bungalows, now bleached and ruinous, yet whose names live on in the streets—Carter Road, Perry Road. Those who grew up before independence recall their resentment of the white children in the schools, often their academic inferiors, but taking precedence over them in everything. 'Whenever there was a parade, they always stood in front of us, they always presented the flowers, made the speeches of welcome. After 1942, what pleasure it gave us to follow them, shouting 'Quit India' after them in the streets.'

Yet the lives of the people were deeply marked, not only by the manners and habits of the country they had never seen, but also by its artcfacts and products, many of which were imported specifically to replace broken traditions and discontinued indigenous practice. 'Our stainless steel cutlery came from Sheffield, our plates were from Stoke-on-Trent. Our shoes were Lilley and Skinner, we ate Chivers' jelly, Bird's Custard, Crosse and Blackwell soup. We were more familiar with the geography of manufacture in Britain than we were with our own country.' The crockery stacked on the dresser, some of it inherited from grandparents, is stamped 'Adams semi-porcelain, Burslem'. Indeed, their whole lives were articulated to Britain. 'When Grandma did her City and Guild examination in dressmaking, all her work, her designs, had to go to London for approval. In fact her work was highly commended, so much so that the examiners kept it.'

Not surprisingly, some older people remember the British with nostalgia. 'At least they kept order. There were no slums in Bombay then. They gave us discipline. People never locked their doors.' As one woman said, 'Life was safe, as long as you accepted your subordination as black people. If that was a good life, then I suppose you might miss it. But for most of us, it was intolerable.'

In the old Portuguese village of Panwar, you can still see the remains of the solid dry stone walls that mark the emplacement of the original colonial structures. Some of the houses have fallen into ruin, and have not been rebuilt—regulations now require a greater distance between the structures. There is no traffic, apart from bicycles, an occasional autorickshaw in the narrow lanes. It is an enclave of antique rustic quaintness amid the chaos and pollution of Bombay, where women come with headloads of fish, fruit and vegetables and cry their wares from house to house.

Hermann and Vinita occupy the upper portion of Hermann's family house. It is cool and spacious, reached by a stairway in wood with carved balustrade and gallery. Hermann recently discovered the diary of his great-grandfather; and it affords a glimpse of the sensibility of those already long colonized, but hovering between the Portuguese and British traditions. Written in perfect copperplate handwriting, it begins in the 1850s, and moves between the two colonial languages with great fluency, and it is pierced by a sense of loss that extends far beyond the record of the premature deaths of those he loved. The early pages are poems, written when he was a child; and later becomes a register of the deaths of siblings and relatives, and revealing how precarious life was on this swampy and malarial coast. Later, it records the taxes paid to the British, the money he lent, and inventories of the dowries he provided for his daughters. A poem about Bandra dates from 1857:

> Oh loved Bandra ever bright and fair,
> Thy gentle zephyrs and salubrious air!
> Thy silent groves and woods of lofty palm,
> How pleasant here to roam in evening's calm.

As the number of deaths increases, the mood becomes more sombre. 'The Almighty God was pleased to call my mother from this world into another on Sunday 27th April 1856 at about one o'clock p.m. . . .' '10th April 1856; The Almighty God was pleased to remove my brother Manooly who was about four years of age.' 'There is an hour when I must die, nor do I know when it will come. A thousand children such as I are called by death to their doom.'

> Let me improve the hours while I live
> Before the day of grace is fled.
> There's no repentance in the grave
> No pardon offered to the dead.

He was employed 'by Dr Wilson's school as a teacher from October 1858, at a salary of Rupees 3 a month'. As he grows older, the entries are more and more sparse; he laconically notes that the title of Empress of India was given to Queen Victoria on 1st July 1877, among entries recording 'the amount of government tax to be paid to the following persons from whom I have bought fields.' There is a note of money lent at ten per cent per annum, the dates of birth of his children, and the dates of the death of many of them not long afterwards.

The majority of people in Bandra remained poor during the colonial period, even though many were educated by the British for minor posts in the administration. They benefited eventually from the fact that small family farms came to be enclosed by the city of Bombay, and the rising value of even the smallest parcel of land in a crowded city, much of the terrain of which had been reclaimed from the sea. Melanie's father came from the island of Gorai to live in Mazgaon, the docks area of Bombay. Because his family spoke Portuguese, he failed his English examination, and went as an apprentice weaver in one of the mills, then being constructed in Bombay in the style of those in Lancashire. He was paid five rupees per month. The cloth from the mill had to be sent to Manchester to be printed, and was then re-exported to Bombay. He later rose to be mill manager, and eventually became the first Indian head of the Victoria Jubilee Textile Institute. His son became the first mayor of Bandra, then a municipality still separate from Bombay. He distinguished himself by abolishing the night-soil system, and by the introduction of modern sanitation and street-lighting. 'Of course the lamp-lighters used to steal the oil and sell it, with the result that all the street-lights would go out in the middle of the night.' In the 1920s, he and a group of prominent fellow-citizens donated their own land and bought from others, in order to start a co-operative building society. 'They went to the Collector and said "You take money in taxes, yet people are still dying of plague."' They built a model suburb, a school and hospital. Each house was in a compound of 1,000 square yards, and had to be at least twenty-five yards from the road. Many of these are now overgrown, shaded by casuarina, acacia and palms; the paint is peeling and the concrete has been stained by the years of violent monsoon. Other houses have been demolished, and blocks of expensive flats built, with a veneer of ceramic and marble, and a uniformed guard at the gate.

The tenacity of colonial penetration is, of course, sometimes more malign than mere archaic and ceremonious manners. Some people have internalized a racial snobbery which expresses itself in advertisements for marriage-partners in the Times of India, demanding 'wheaten complexion' or 'fair skin'. Others have identified with the colonial culture to such a degree that they have smothered their own Indian identity. Edgar is now thirty-five. His father, as a child, was bonded in labour to a big landowner in Konkan, sold by his own landless father to keep the family from starvation. When he had worked out the years of his bondage, he joined the Indian army, and fought in the war of 1939–45. He then returned to Mangalore, and worked as a woodcutter, later leaving for Bombay to find work as a dock labourer. Edgar was born in Bandra: they lived in a hut which nobody else wanted because it had been the scene of a gruesome murder. Although Edgar's mother spoke Konkani, she insisted on his getting an English education. He speaks perfect English, but grew up without any real knowledge of his mother-tongue. He did his BA, and is now studying for an MA in English Literature. Married now, he lives in a *jopadpatti*, a hut in a slum, with his wife, his three children, and his parents. He works as a typewriter salesman, and studies in the evening. The set books he must study are *King Lear*, *Dubliners* and *The Heart of Darkness*. He is passionate about the condition of the poor in Indian society, about social justice. He wants to write about social issues, but he feels he must perfect his English before he will have the confidence to set pen to paper. 'How is my English?' he asks. He has spoken English all his life, but has never before had a proper conversation with anyone from Britain. He laments that nobody reads English anymore in India. 'Nobody reads Jane Austen. They don't even read P.G. Wodehouse.' The conflict between the poverty of his backgound and the experience of higher education has been very traumatizing. He even went to a psychiatrist, because he felt there was something wrong with him, in his inability to reconcile his love of English with his concern for the poor.

Many younger people have reacted against such extreme patterns of domination. Most want their children to grow up fluent in Marathi and Hindi, although English remains the first language of the East Indians. Some of them are ironic now about the role of their parents, calling them *chamchas* of the British, literally meaning 'spoons', and indicating an extreme servility which the new generation is free from. But the conflicts remain, snobberies persist. One man, a model of an English gentleman, maintains a house in England, which he visits for the month of May, because of the London season, and to avoid the heat of the Bombay pre-monsoon period; one woman stopped eating and died, because she had given birth only to daughters, and her husband had taunted her with her inability to provide him with a son.

Not all East Indians are affluent. Rosy is a domestic servant. Formerly, she would clean up to eight houses a day, but now, at fifty-five, she works in only three. Her employers are members of the church's Social Justice Movement, and they pay her well. This has made some of their neighbours angry—they accuse them of distorting the market by paying more than the going rate. Rosy lives in a small hut, ten feet by twelve. It is neat and well-kept, with a stone floor and a fan. Her husband, a former railway worker, is now retired. Rosy, perhaps in keeping with some ancient idea of propriety, does not name her husband to outsiders, but refers to him as 'Uncle'. She gets up at four thirty in the morning to get water, because by the time she reaches home at night the water is turned off. She was one of eight children, four girls and four boys. She started work when she was eight, cleaning and sweeping, for one rupee a month. The family had a small plot of land, one hour's journey from Bombay; they were self-sufficient in vegetables and rice. Rosy has no outings and no holidays, apart from a yearly visit of one week to her village. Her two sons are both working, in hotels and catering. They have entered a more institutionalized form of service in the modern sector of the economy, and are therefore considered to have risen in the world.

After independence, many East Indians reached prominence in national affairs. I went to a party, held to celebrate the engagement of two young people from well-known Bandra families. They are sufficiently emancipated to be able to laugh at their grandparents' stories of solemn and elaborate marriage-broking, where the dowry was spread out for inspection, and wily elders scraped the gold pots with a stone to discover that they were really made of brass, with gold-leaf veneer, and called the wedding off. Among the guests at the party were a woman who had been personal assistant to the US ambassador, the editor of a national newspaper, the man who had been Information Minister at the time of Mrs Gandhi's Emergency, Sanjay Gandhi's former flying instructor, the General who had been in charge of Delhi at the time of Emergency, and of Kashmir in the Indo-Pak war. That this urbane and anglicized people grew out of families of toddy-tappers, potters and fishing people who inhabited these unhealthy, marshy shores (and some of the fishing families remain, squeezed onto a narrow strip of land beside the sea, still laying out their bombils and sardines on the sand to dry) offers a subject for wonder at the infinite malleability of the human sensibility. If they are uneasy at the rise of Shiv Sena—and Bal Thackeray, its leader, lives at Bandra—they do not show it. They remain, a secure and devout community, protected by their dignity and pride, their strict morality, against external change. And here is a paradox; that very malleability becomes, with time, extremely rigid, ossified and no longer open. Perhaps their position indicates something of the very violent force with which the alien values were imposed upon them in the first place, and of the attachment of people to an imposed identity when their own has been so deeply impaired. Their resistance to the next wave of colonial penetration—the primacy of money and the exaltation of market values—may also make of them allies of those in the West who are resisting the same forces of penetration into our own culture.

The sunsets over the mangroves along the Bandra shoreline are spectacular. When the tide goes out, the rocks are pink, and silver pools hold captive the fading light of the sky. Some milky wisps of cirrus deepen to orange, and the palm-leaves clatter on the languid arc of their branches in the warm wind. When a flock of seabirds starts up from a rock, black in the dusk, it seems as though the rock itself has shattered and burst into the air. The sun breaks into the water like a spilt yolk, and then the rocks lose their colour; everything solidifies in the dying light. Up and down the sea-road the young men in Maruti cars, with tinted windows and loudspeakers playing Madonna and Paul Simon, fly over the speedbreakers, throwing up clouds of dust into the faces of the sedate elderly women out for an evening stroll.

A final picture from Bombay. It is late afternoon at Nanachowk, close to Grant Road station. The black smoke from the traffic exhausts stagnates in the hot air, forming a permanent metallic haze. A small procession of men is walking on the road. At their head, a man, perhaps in his mid-thirties, is holding a bundle in a palmyra mat. His hands are outstretched before him under this slender burden, as though in supplication. The bundle is the body of a small child, wrapped in cerements and covered with the petals of marigolds and jasmine, which spill, flakes of yellow, onto the burning road.

He walks steadily in the glare of afternoon, followed by ten or a dozen others. Their faces are quite impassive. No one stops to look at the little procession, no doubt too common a sight in this city to be worthy of attention. As a diesel lorry passes, a gust of dark smoke envelops the man and his precious cargo. Very slightly, he veers away from the traffic, holding the child's body aside, as though to avoid contamination by the fumes. Behind him, buses and taxis hoot impatiently, but he does not quicken his step. The meaning of his posture is not difficult to discern: it is the attitude of someone making an offering; his child is a human sacrifice, a part of the costs of a form of development that brings, with economic growth, the stunting and extinction of humanity.

8/ FROM DINDOSHI TO EASTERHOUSE

THE LANDSCAPES COULDN'T BE more different: in the mono-
chrome grey of Glasgow's biggest housing scheme, scoured by
Atlantic winds, everything is hard and unyielding, stone, concrete, metal
and glass. There could be no greater contrast than with Dindoshi: a place
of relentless sun, bare red-brown rocks, sparse, thorny vegetation, dust
swirling around the uneven self-built structures. At first sight, these might
appear to be alien and mutually incomprehensible settlements. Yet both
communities bear the same stigmata of those who must live off the fag-end
of market economies; and accordingly, there is more to unite than to
separate them.

Both are on the far edge of industrial cities. The tall buildings of the
centres can be seen, slabs of gleaming marble by day, glittering with lights
after dark. The hills beyond the city boundaries are also visible, capped
with late-winter snow beyond Glasgow, fresh and cool in Bombay, where
the protected trees of the wild park look down on the exposed slum area.
Both are places to which people have been removed from central areas,
where their presence had become an embarrassment—in the Northern
city from the slums of the Gorbals, in the Southern one from the pavements of Bombay Central. In Glasgow, people had lived close to the
traditional—and now decayed—heavy industry along the Clyde; the
Bombay slumdwellers had set up their shelters from where they could
service the rich—industrial work, but also domestic labour, construction
work and street-vending. When the people were forcibly removed to Dindoshi, they were given small plots of land, for which they pay rent, and
which gives them the right to stay there only as long as the Corporation
sees fit. There is little work, either in Easterhouse or Dindoshi; to make

a living, people must travel long distances, which adds to the stress of living in unhealthy conditions.

Both communities have similar complaints. The work available is not only distant, but is often low-paid, de-skilled and demeaning. People leave for Bombay at five or six in the morning. A bus journey is followed by an hour in the train, which is so intolerably overcrowded that every day there are accidents, when people clinging to the open doors fall and are killed. Because the employment structure of Glasgow has been so radically modified, the people of Easterhouse find themselves doing similar work to their counterparts in Dindoshi—service industries, low paid self-employment, selling, some of it in the informal economy. Unemployment in both areas has had a similar effect—it makes a job, any job, at almost any price, something to be coveted, no matter how damaging the product, no matter what the conditions of work. People from Easterhouse are working in catering, in clothing factories, doing assembly work, security work, cleaning, working for the local authority. It is scarcely surprising that the stories from the people of Bombay echo those of their unacknowledged kindred in Glasgow; if Zamida tells of the hopelessness of ten hours at a bench soldering, Cathy will speak of bursting into tears with frustration at the futility of feeding leaves into a machine that makes cigars all day long. Tony, in Glasgow, worked all day in a clothing factory, staying on to work through the night and then doing his next day's shift too. Rafiq has also frequently worked through the night, in order to finish an urgent export order of shirts to Europe. If Pat recalls her mother catching the first bus into the city at five a.m. to do cleaning in offices, and dying of a heart attack at the age of forty-three, Aruna also crosses her city every day to clean three houses in the wealthy district of Malabar Hill, but because she is no longer young, she can command only the lowest rate for the job. Fatima left her family to work as a servant in the Gulf, and sent money home from Bahrain for three years; just as David went to work in the construction industry in Birmingham, remitting money to the wife and children he rarely saw. Prakash runs a drinks stall on Marine Drive, Sunil cleans at the Oberoi Towers hotel, and both are away from their home more than twelve hours a day; similarly, Jean does two cleaning jobs in the city centre; because of the bus fares, she spends the period between work in the library or drinking tea in a cafe. She is away from home fourteen hours a day.

Many people in Dindoshi are self-employed; selling vegetables or fruit from a hand-cart, setting up a small booth for cigarettes, a tailoring business with nothing but an ancient Singer sewing-machine. In Easterhouse, many must now fall back on similar practices; the estate is full of old vans and run-down buses that have been painted up and turned into mobile shops, selling confectionery, bread, sweets, cigarettes, ice-cream. They patrol the streets until eleven o'clock at night, attracting custom with chiming bells. Others have set up second-hand clothing businesses, doing alterations or mending, undertaking electrical repairs. Children deliver tomorrow's *Daily Record* at ten thirty in the evening; just as the young news-vendors are out on the streets of Bombay, weaving in and out of the traffic until the early hours of the morning.

The absence of amenities at Dindoshi makes life there resemble the conditions of those living on the edge of survival in Glasgow, as the caring fabric of the welfare state wears away; the young people no longer able to claim benefit run away from home, or lodge unofficially with whoever will take them in; the people who have flitted to avoid debt, living by begging or borrowing, having recourse to prostitution if all else fails them. In Bombay, people exhibit their mutilations and sores to move passers-by to compassion; in the cities of Britain, children sit on the stations with placards round their necks, declaring themselves hungry or homeless. The stories of high mortality and avoidable death are strikingly similar. The bitter observation came repeatedly from Glasgow, rather than Bombay, that 'life is cheap here'—lives that could have been saved if the ambulance had got there sooner, if the harassed doctor had been a little more attentive, if the people weren't exhausted and prematurely aged by the time they're forty; while the memories of TB, undernourishment, of the early orphanings of so many children are still everyday experience at Dindoshi.

The escape stories from unbearable social conditions echo each other —alcohol and drugs represent the easiest way out in both communities. In Bombay, as in Glasgow, children are sniffing solvents—butane lighter-fuel in Easterhouse, 'solution' in Dindoshi, which is a powerful glue. 'Brown sugar', a highly impure form of heroin, is readily available to the young in Bombay; whereas in Glasgow, heroin has become rare, because the quality had been so adulterated that its purpose was defeated. A sleeping capsule called tomazipan—'yellow eggs' or 'jelly-babies', as they are familiarly called, are popular now, over-prescribed by doctors, and sometimes sold by patients who are desperate for money. More widespread is the use of alcohol—whether made from jaggery in illicit stills in Dindoshi, vitiated by battery fluid, or whether homebrew, fortified with industrial alcohol. The betting-shop in Glasgow has its analogue in the card-games of chance of the young unemployed men all over Dindoshi.

Moneylenders play a similar role in both places. Living on the periphery is always more expensive than living in centrally-located slums. In Bombay, many families have gone into debt to buy materials for house-construction —metal, wood, sacking; in Easterhouse, to buy furniture or bedding. In Easterhouse, the people who most need help from the social fund are those most likely to be refused, because they have no hope of repaying the loan. The respectable end of the private loans market—and many in Easterhouse have their Provident books—shows that a loan of £500 will cost £830 if paid back over a period of 100 weeks. Unofficial loans are extortionate, and the loan companies less squeamish about the means they employ to recover bad debts. In Dindoshi, people may sell their cooking vessels, pawn wedding-jewellery in order to start up in self-employment, or for the sake of a wedding, or a visit to the home-village—debts at such a rate of interest that they may never again be free of the moneylenders.

As is also to be expected, resistance to social and economic oppression is tending to converge in both places, outside and beyond existing political parties, and more often than not, led by women. In Easterhouse, one group, Cathy, Pat, Beatrice and Marie, have been involved in a survey designed to demonstrate the relationship between damp and mould in houses and the health of both children and adults. They have also been offered money from the EEC (European Economic Community) for a unique tenants' initiative to heat and insulate badly constructed homes; only the reluctance of the city authorites to match the EEC grant is preventing the scheme from going ahead. In Dindoshi, some of the women residents are fighting for the right to buy a plot of land from the municipality, because only then will the poor have real security against eviction by those more powerful; they have also set up a co-operative of women, sewing and manufacturing, and marketing their own products.

The fight for basic health care at Dindoshi—safe water and drainage, which is the surest method of preventing childhood disease—is paralleled by the struggle in Glasgow against the decay of existing services. Cathy tells how water from the tap became cloudy and foul-smelling; later, feathers appeared when she turned on the water. A pigeon had drowned in the water tank. In Dindoshi, the children sit and play where the waste water collects in the hollows, drinking it when they are thirsty, with the inevitable consequence of debilitating sickness and diarrhoea.

The people from the central areas of Glasgow were removed because their homes had become 'unfit for human habitation'; no-one, however, has cast doubt upon the humanity of the rich, who now occupy the renovated tenements which were not torn down in the 1960s and 1970s. In Bombay, the land on which the poor were living had become too valuable for them to remain there. Even so, they are not permitted undisputed occupancy of the sometime wasteland onto which they have been transferred. What they call in India 'economically more powerful classes' are moving in. At Dindoshi, many people cannot afford the rents, so they have (illegally, of course) sold their plots to richer people, who have built more substantial houses, opened shops and businesses. The poor have gone back to live on pavements from which they were evicted, where they can at least earn a living of sorts. This has its equivalent in Glasgow, where the council has sold parts of Easterhouse to private developers for renovation and sale. Some of the flats have been refurbished and sold; a few of them, it is true, to local people, but many to those who will spend no more than a year or two there, before selling at a considerable profit, none of which will bring any benefit to the community.

The victims of economic oppression are invariably blamed, not only for their own poverty, but for all kinds of other evils. Easterhouse has— quite unjustly—inherited the kind of reputation that formerly clung to the inner-city slum areas. It is seen as a kind of human rubbish-dump, of people who are idlers, winos and no-hopers. The same reaction is provoked by the people who have come from the sidewalks of Bombay—they are said to be criminals and prostitutes, they have come to the city for the bright lights or for easy pickings, even though it should be clear to those who say these things that bright lights never yet nourished a family, and the city is too hard for easy pickings. The truth is, in both cases, that the people are performing indispensable functions in the urban economy. At Easterhouse, they absorbed the human costs of the restructuring of

Britain, and have been dutifully 'pricing themselves into jobs', as they have been urged to do; even if this means working for ninety-nine pence an hour as security guard, working every night and all week-end, sewing, machining, soldering, going into domestic service, cleaning and selling.

It isn't so much that Britain now has its enclaves of 'Third World' poverty. It is rather, the natural consequence of an increasingly integrated, single global economy, where people in regions all over the world are pitted competitively against each other. Common patterns of exploitation and suffering are more and more visible. And for all the difference in environment, culture, colour and religion, there is a dawning sense of a shared predicament. Indeed, many people described Easterhouse as 'a township', 'barracks'—echoing the Hammonds'* description of the early industrial period, 'South Africa with only economic apartheid'. It may be that new and more hopeful solidarities are in the process of being formed. People in Dindoshi and Easterhouse for instance, are in communication, sharing their common problems; and although this is only a pin-prick, it is being replicated in similar places all over the world which recognize the same patterns of exploitation and pain across those increasingly fragile national boundaries that do nothing to halt the spread of levelling global forces. Perhaps a new and truly transnational phase in the struggle for social justice is only just beginning.

* J. L. & Barbara Hammond, *The Town Labourer*, (Longman, Green, London, 1925)

9 / THE HOPES OF EASTERHOUSE: MOBILIZING THE POOR

CERTAIN PLACES BECOME ASSOCIATED with great suffering—Whitechapel, the Rhondda, the Gorbals; more recently, Liverpool 8 and Handsworth. To this list we may perhaps add Easterhouse, on the edge of Glasgow, a township the size of Perth, a vast public housing 'scheme', as they are called in Scotland. Its earlier reputation for violence and gang warfare has died away now, to be replaced with the image of resigned desolation, more appropriate to the 1980s. This is where the cameras come for documentaries on Thatcher's Britain. This is where the Sun reporters made for, with their telephoto lenses, to take pictures of what they called 'the worst estate in Europe'.

There is indeed poverty. The prospect from Wardie Street, in the heart of Easterhouse, is not welcoming. On a cold February afternoon, the icy wind lashes out of a metal-grey sky. The patches of grass are muddy and lifeless; rain trembles in silver buds on skeletal saplings.

The people, too, shrink against the cold; youngsters pull down the sleeves of jumpers over their hands, heads sink into thin windcheaters, women clutch coats around themselves, purse in hand—a frieze of impoverished and defeated humanity. Sometimes, it seems, the people have become an incarnation of an ideology that tells them that poverty is their own fault. It is as though they had accepted that deprivation and unemployment were indeed all that they deserved of life; had permitted socially-produced ills to conceal themselves behind flawed individuals. The stories of self-inflicted violence, of destructive addictions to drink and drugs suggest a self-esteem so impaired that many have taken to punishing themselves, imposing upon themselves the severe moral judgement that emanates from the rich and powerful.

Talking to people here, you swiftly gain an impression of high mortality, avoidable illness, early death: a brother's suicide, a father's death at work at the age of forty. Marie Knox, in whose flat I am staying, has had three heart attacks; her husband died of cancer in his early forties. One evening, Eleanor, Marie's grand-daughter arrives, asking for a suit-case for her boy-friend who is to be admitted to hospital. As a child, this boy was turned out of the house by his father; after wandering all night in the rain, he caught pneumonia and lost a lung. Now his remaining lung is infected. The bus journey to hospital will take one and a half hours; it isn't considered sufficiently urgent for an ambulance. A neighbour recalls how, when she sent for the ambulance, her mother stopped breathing, was revived by a policeman, but died again before the ambulance arrived. Marie herself lost both parents when she was four.

Many commentators have observed what they call the 'apathy' of places like Easterhouse; but this is an inadequate description of what is really a watchful retreat from social and political discussions that do not touch their pain, the only rational response to their feeling of impotence. But this feeling is, in turn, giving way to a growing anger. The question is being asked, in something louder than a murmur, how the sense of powerlessness is compatible with the cherished freedoms we are supposed to enjoy. Indeed, talk of the break-up of the United Kingdom is something more than idle speculation here. In the last district council election, only twelve per cent of the people cast their vote.

The years of what people are now openly calling 'economic oppression' have brought forth another, more vigorous response in the community. Cathy McCormack is a passionate woman in her thirties, committed to the kind of radical change which is believed, in more fashionable areas, to have been struck from the agenda. She speaks with energy and an authority that comes from having known despair during the seven years that she and Tony, her husband, have been out of work. 'I was so broken by it that I felt there was no point in living. I wanted to go to sleep and never wake up again. Then one day, something happened. It was a kind of awakening, almost a spiritual experience.' Cathy realized that nothing was ever going to happen, that no one was going to rescue them. 'I understood that my life is here, in this place, and no fantasy of escape would help. This is where the wains must grow up and make their lives, here we must survive or perish together.'

The achievements of the groups with which Cathy McCormack has worked, are impressive. What began as a modestly-titled 'Dampness Group' in 1982, led to the first tenants' initiative in proposing an energy-saving programme of renovation for cold damp houses to have been offered a grant from the EEC. The tenants held what they called a 'Heat-fest', where groups of architects, academics, students and tenants devised the most effective means of remedying the defects of houses that had been built with substandard bricks, where it was assumed that coal-fires would heat the houses. The winning design suggested cladding and injecting blown-glass into the brick cavities; double-glazing the verandas and inserting solar panels in the roof. This would bring down the cost of heating each flat adequately to £5 a week, saving up to £1,000 a year on each apartment. The District Council had promised to find the money to top up the EEC grant. The group heard nothing for several months, until June 1989, when they met with a brusque refusal from the council.

The Health Group took part in a survey in three cities, published in June 1989, linking dampness and mould in flats to the health of both children and adults. There is confirmation in the report of what Cathy McCormack calls common sense—that the presence of dampness and fungal spores in houses contributes to coughing, wheezes and vomiting in children, as well as nausea, breathlessness and fainting in adults, and that the graph for adult and child disorders in houses that were damp followed the same line. A microbiologist found that some dwellings were harbouring up to fifteen different kinds of mould, producing allergenic or toxic reactions, lesions in the respiratory tract, saprophytic colonies on mucus plugs, inflammation and irritation of the nose, bronchial passages and alveoli. The report was launched at a press conference in the House of Commons, and three representatives of the people from Glasgow who had taken part were present. It was impossible not to be aware of how the tenants, usually extremely articulate and strong in their advocacy of the case for the deprived, were overcome by the grandeur of the setting and the fluency of the professionals and MPs. The Health Group intends to research into the link between heart disease and cold stress. The Healthy Cities Project in Glasgow is conducting a campaign that is aimed at the reduction of heart disease in the city. The Health Group takes issue with the insistence that diet, exercise and smoking are the sole factors: 'It's also unhealthy living conditions. By telling people to go jogging and to eat brown bread, you make it *their* problem, and offer individual remedies. We know that damp cold housing is also a contributory cause.'

The physical environment is harsh and unwelcoming. As you turn into the wind on Wardie Street, there is no shelter; the women's umbrellas turn inside out, hoods of anoraks are blown down, faces freeze in a stinging sleety rain, and the wind fills the prams that shelter bonneted babies. Even inside the houses, you can't get warm: draughts set the curtains dancing, there are quarrels over who is to sit closest to the fire; there is fear of turning up the heat, because of fuel debt and the bill for the coldest quarter of the year. Breath condenses in icy bathrooms, and clothes are damp by morning, exhaling a faint musty smell of mildew. The teapot simmers permanently on the stove, alternating with cups of hot Oxo. The chapped hands of women bleed from being plunged so many times in cold water; they grimace, but do not complain.

'The truth is that a quarter of a million people in Glasgow live at or below the level of state benefit. In Easterhouse, twice as many mothers lose their babies at birth as in the most prosperous parts of the city, two and a half times as many children die here as in the middle-class suburb of Bearsden; three times as many children have low birthweight. Forty-five per cent of those in work are doing low-paid jobs. Why don't all those who write about how awful Easterhouse is give support to the people who are trying to do something about it?'

The question that keeps recurring here is, 'How did the dream of Easterhouse turn into such a nightmare?' Those who came here from the Gorbals or Govan in the 1950s speak of their delight at having their own front door, of seeing open fields and farmland. 'The promised land', 'paradise', were words they used then. But a new generation has grown up here to another kind of poverty than that represented by the single-ends (one-room tenements), with bed and 'jaw-box' (sink) in the same room, shared toilets with such wide cracks in the door, that in the interests of modesty, people had to hold a newspaper against them.

Easterhouse has been overtaken by social and economic change unforeseen by those who planned it. Indeed, its very existence was a pledge that there would never be a return to the poverty and mass unemployment of the 1930s. (Alas, nothing was promised about the modernized versions of these things that were to haunt the 1980s.) During the 1950s and 1960s, the defects of the housing were masked by full employment and cheap fuel. 'The buses used to be full leaving Easterhouse every morning. Now, the only rush hour is of the social workers coming in to service the place, and leaving at five.' It is the supreme irony that Easterhouse embodied the very change of environment thought to ensure that the old social evils would never return; yet there they are, showing through the threadbare change of scenery—and some new ones as well.

Rena Raillie came as a teenager with her family from the Gorbals. 'The whole thing fell apart, because they never tackled social justice. They just built more elegant barracks. It isn't charity that we want but justice. The professionals who come in from outside live off our poverty—the doctors and carers, officials, social workers and salespeople.' (I met the same reaction in Bombay from communities who referred to the social workers and animators and academics who thrive on them as 'the pimps of poverty'.) 'They draw their income from our poverty, but they spend it outside. That's why so many of them blame the poor—they daren't look at their own interest in the maintenance of poverty. They needn't worry—a system that is based on injustice cannot be reformed; and reform is about as far as the imagination of even the most enlightened will stretch.'

Yvonne is in her thirties. She spent her childhood in care in the English Midlands. Her husband's family came from Glasgow, but he has now left her to look after the two boys. She felt stranded in Easterhouse, with no living relative but the children. Out of her £33.60 a week, with £14.50 child allowance, she is paying back £13 a week out of the £281 her husband removed from the gas meter before his final departure. 'His leaving present', as she says. The local shopkeeper allows her credit, but things are expensive in the small shops, and as soon as she gets her money on Mondays, she has to hand most of it over for items already consumed and forgotten. 'Poverty means every day is the same. Choice means eating or being cold. It means not realizing it was your birthday until it was over.' Yvonne took part in a television discussion about poverty, and discovered that she was wonderfully eloquent. For some people, a by-product of being unemployed has been the finding of talents and abilities they didn't know they possessed.

Tony is a skilled tailor. He has tried to start his own business several times, but the cost of travelling to fit, measure and deliver was too much. He had a market stall with a friend, but they lost money. He wanted to start a clothing repairs and alterations business on the Enterprise Allowance, but couldn't raise the £1,000 required in order to start up. In his anger, he has begun to write poetry, deeply felt, about the woman who lives in terror that the Social Services will take her children away because she cannot afford to look after them properly, about the youngster whose home is a cardboard box. Other poems are satiric: a rejoinder to the Glasgow City of Culture Campaign begins:

> The city of culture
> that's a laugh
> We have it growing
> in the bath.
> On the ceiling, on the walls,
> it's even growing in the hall.

Tony's mother died of TB when he was four. Her husband was left with four step-children; Tony was farmed out to an aunt and uncle. His real father had been killed by a hit-and-run driver. If Tony is angry, his anger comes not from self-pity, but is directed outwards, at a society that damages and destroys people, as he has seen happen in his lifetime. He insists that when people relate their personal story, this is part of a continuing, collective epic of dispossession that has afflicted the people of Scotland for many generations. When he says 'Human life is cheap here', such words are not idle, but rise from an experience of bereavements and mutilations, the sufferings of loved flesh and blood.

Cathy also writes. Brought up a Catholic, she is saddened that there seems to be no greeting in the Church for the poor. Recently, she wrote *A Letter to God*, which begins

> Dear God, I don't know how I am ever going to post this letter to you. I still go to your house on Sunday, but you never seem to be in. Have you changed your address? When I was a wee girl, you were always at home. I really looked forward to my visit each week.

Rodd Cherry has been out of work for seven years. A building labourer, he lost his job in the public spending cuts of the early eighties. He kept his sanity by going fishing. Some of the youngsters from the estate went with him, and they started a club. Since then, he has been working voluntarily with young people, especially those who have turned to the consolation of drugs.

> Young girls have a baby to give them a purpose in life. For young men, there's nothing. The community supports are not there. Those who dismiss talk of the loss of community as nostalgia are doing a disservice to the people who've suffered from that loss; they serve the purposes of those who want to make money out of the powerlessness and the isolation of the young—the drug pushers, the brewers, the peddlers of dreams. When I see some of them walking through Barlanark, heads hung low, hands in pockets, they look like Lowry's matchstick men. I watch them, on make-work schemes, picking up paper and litter, washing the closes. They call it training, I call it humiliation. Training is what they give them instead of education. Training is for circus animals, not people.
>
> We used to live in the city centre. My Granny was one of the original Littlewood's pools winners—£47,000. She bought an apartment in a house that once belonged to a doctor. But all the houses were pulled down. The city clearances were the same as the Highland clearances—move the people out, because they want to use the land for more profitable purposes.

If drugs have damaged many young people, the effects of alcohol have been even more corrosive, because more widespread. Alice Alexander, who has seen her husband, David, through the worst that alcohol can do, says 'Is alcoholism a social problem? Is it the fault of individuals, or of the brewing and drug companies that have to go on selling more and more of their products to keep profits rising?' David is now thirty-four. He started drinking at fourteen, long before he left school. He drank for nearly fifteen years before he recognized that he was alcoholic. He has now been cured for four years, but his health has been irreparably damaged.

The flat is well-furnished—black carpet, white walls, black and white striped three-piece suite, a lantern-style lampshade. David is now permanently on invalidity benefit, and in constant pain from the damaged pancreas. 'Alcohol was my life,' he explains. 'Without it, you feel you've nothing. The removal of alcohol leaves a void in your life; it's like losing someone close to you. I'm fit for nothing now. All I do is watch televison.' David went to his doctor for depression before he recognized his addiction to alcohol. The doctor prescribed Ativan, and he became dependent on that too. Later, after he had been in a psychiatric clinic to be dried out, he again went to his doctor, again for depression, and Ativan was prescribed once more. David began work at fifteen as a clerk with Glasgow Corporation; but was then offered a job as apprentice to a terrazza and tile-layer. But he had become too fond of drinking, so he left it to go hod-carrying with a mate who was a fellow-drinker. He moved to Birmingham; tax-free money, more to spend on booze, nobody from home to see what you were doing.

He came back to Glasgow, worked as a labourer, but was drinking more and more. He was quite unable to recognize his alcoholism. 'You think you're in control, you can beat it if you want to, but by that time it's running you.' Alice says 'Deep in myself, I always knew there was hope for him. But in the end, I had to call the police and kick him out of the flat. But instead of bringing him to his senses, he went and booked into a hostel, and really finished up on Skid Row.' 'I used to eat at soup kitchens. I neglected myself, became scruffy and filthy.' Alice made a separate claim for herself and the two children from Social Security, because she knew he would always be back asking her for money. The DHSS hounded her, waiting outside in the mornings, always knocking on the door to see if David was there. 'They thought we'd split up just to get more money out of them.'

The last drinking bout triggered pancreatitis; it wasn't until then, when he was lying in intensive care, that David realized the harm he'd done. 'They've told me that if I have another drink, it'll be the end of me. The damage is irreversible.'

David was brought up by his grandmother. He never knew his father. He called his grandmother his 'wee mother', and was very attached to her. 'But it was a strange childhood. She and the man she was married to never spoke to each other for ten years. Not a word. Christmas Day was just like any other. Complete silence. My wee mother died the day Alice and I were married.'

Alice, too, has had a hard life. Her brother went to London for work, was in prison and died of drink; her sister also died in her early thirties, 'maybe drugs'. 'I had to believe in David, hang on to him to bring him back to me. I've lost too many others. The system fucks people up, and then somebody makes profit out of them when they try to escape from their misery.'

Michael Docherty is in his thirties, and was out of work for six years. He is now a supervisor on an Employment Training scheme. His parents came here from Govan.

> Easterhouse was then a dormitory town for Singer, Beardmore, Parkhead Forges. It was to serve an industry that has now gone. That time looks like a golden age from where we are now. There was a lot of gang activity at that time. Frankie Vaughan came here to 'rescue' young people from violence. There was a lot of publicity which made people angry. But at least people were alive and reacting then. The eerie silence that hangs over privatized pain is like a social death. It isn't just unemployment. A much deeper violence has been done to the people of Scotland. Easterhouse is a township. Like Soweto. Economic oppression is more efficient than racial oppression—this is why the South African capitalists want an end to apartheid. Economic oppression looks more innocent when it's colour-blind. Economic oppression then looks more random, it can more easily be represented as the fault of the oppressed: when they're all one colour, you can't do that.

The difference from Soweto, however, he acknowledges, is that in Soweto they know the meaning of solidarity. That isn't to say that Easterhouse doesn't have its militant people. But there are two communities here—'the activists and the rest; the latter are the community that society has forgotten. Yet the community groups are all that stand between the poorest and even worse levels of exploitation.'

Michael Docherty is a single parent. He says that the macho culture of Easterhouse is an illusion. To forbid men to express their vulnerability and their pain is yet another violence against them; and this results in even greater anger against women and children; and against themselves too. 'What I hate is the way that people tolerate the intolerable.' He believes that Scotland's independence must come. He calls himself 'non-political', to distance himself from the absence of radical alternatives on offer from mainstream politicians.

At Barlanark Community Centre, Madge, Betty and Jean are celebrating the publication of the book of memories which they and the over-fifty club have produced. They all came here in the early 1950s. Their memories are rooted in the single-end tenements, with infested flock mattresses and scrubbed boards. The key fitted every lock, so the flats were never closed. Nobody, however, they insist, would have set a finger on a child or old person. 'It would have been more than their life was worth.' They say that, as children, 'we didn't want things. We hadn't *learned to want.*' Not that they would wish to go back to it. The notion that the only alternative to what exists now would be a return to the past is very disabling; that there might be another way is obscured by the cloudy and selective memory of the nostalgia industry, just as the clouds of steam obscured everything in the old 'steamies', or wash-houses, which they evoke with such mixed feelings now. Madge put her name down for a flat here ten years before they were built. Betty was lucky—she arranged an exchange with a woman who couldn't bear it here, 'because there was nowhere she could buy fags'. 'We had our own front and back door. You could see for miles. My son was the first baby to be born on the estate. When we came here, I just kept running up and down the stairs. I couldn't believe it, the space, the freedom.' Significantly, their children reject what was heaven to their parents. They say there's nothing to do. 'They want to leave. They think life is somewhere else.' Because older people carry memories of the means test ('The neighbours had given us a loaf and some margarine, so we got nothing'), of the stigma of charity boots and clothing that chafed, they have not lived through the same disillusionment of those who have grown up here, for whom recollections of an older squalor are not still a living experience.

Malcolm Cuthbertson is vicar of the Church of Scotland, St George and St Peter. It is an austere, fortified building at the centre of the Scheme, which has had twelve break-ins within four months. Malcolm says that part of the low sense of self-esteem of the community comes from the fact that it uses up wealth that is produced elsewhere. Little wealth is created here, and that is the greatest crime against a society which sees making money as the highest good. 'Violence here has become inturned; eighty-five per cent of it is domestic, so that people damage those closest to them. The means of escape have also been privatised—television and video, the culture of drugs and drink.

> Hope has to come from within the community. Easterhouse has believed that salvation will come from elsewhere. Initiatives, projects come and go, as they have for thirty years, but the basic situation remains. People here have been items on other people's agendas, other people's ideologies. What is required is actually a liberation struggle. The fact that we live in a democracy has, paradoxically, become a means of stifling dissent—'You live in a democracy, so shut up.' And then, people don't like to acknowledge that they are poor. They see Third World poverty on television, and think 'Well, it's not as bad as that.'

One parishioner said 'We aren't the poor, but we do suffer from poverty.' Malcolm says that the Labour Party is lucky if twenty people turn up for a meeting; the church has two thousand members, and is by far the largest association of people in Easterhouse, and as such, one of the real potential forces for change.

Although many young people say they want to leave Easterhouse, there are many who have never even been to Glasgow. One woman tells how she organized a trip last Christmas, to take a dozen women who had never been off the estate for a Chinese meal and a theatre visit to the city. 'We hired a minibus. On the night, only one woman turned up. We went round the houses, to find out what had happened. At least six told the same story: 'He won't let me.'

It is easy to underestimate those who live here; their energy, their resourcefulness and their intelligence. Cathy remembers how, when she was a child, she was always taught to respect authority.

> I had great reverence for teachers, doctors, priests. I would never open my mouth to contradict anything they said. I wouldn't want

my children to grow up like that. But I suppose the old authority figures are not so strong now. They were only symbols of power and money; and money is now the open symbol of authority, so they don't need the old patriarchal figures. Money talks, and it is obeyed. In a way, it is all more obvious than it used to be. It ought to be easier to fight. But somehow, it isn't.

Late evening. The wind cracks against the stone buildings, shifts the doors on their hinges and the windows in their frames, rattles the dustbin lids. Most of the windows are beaded with condensation. By ten o'clock the grilles are up at the shop windows, and the wind seems to have swept the streets almost completely clear of people. The eerie emptiness of Wardie Street gives it the appearance of being under curfew, a place of occupation by alien forces; and indeed, that is exactly how more and more of those living here are coming to see it.

10 / MARGINALIZING THE POOR

A S THE MARKET ECONOMY GROWS, its claims to be able to eliminate poverty become more convincing, and are supported by the apparent evidence; not only do the materially poor become a minority in the rich world, but they are removed from places where their presence might disturb the possessing classes. Nowhere is this more clear than in the capital of Italy, where the historic centre has been preserved, even though most of those who service it have been evicted.

The romantically named Tor Bella Monaca (Tower of the Beautiful Nun) is beyond the outer ring road on the far eastern periphery of Rome; an estate of some 40,000 people (about the same as Easterhouse), monument to the economic boom of the 1980s, which succeeded in demolishing the last of the shanties and *baracche* that for so many years disfigured the edge of the city.

While excavating the foundations for Bella Monaca, the workmen uncovered a Roman road. The main thoroughfare has been named Via dell' Archeologia. The Roman way runs alongside the buildings in a kind of ditch; a suitable depository for rubbish and waste paper. The setting is dramatic: the bluish hills of Frascati and Tivoli are closer than the city. The most imposing building is the church, a series of huge concrete pillars of declining height that brood over the community, like a set of petrified organ pipes.

The towers of Bella Monaca are without ornament or colour, punitive grey façades with grey shutters. Only geraniums and herbs on the balconies give an indication of the sometime country origin of many of the people—from the Abruzzi, Calabria, Sicily. They used to come to Rome to find work; now, people say, they come to flee violence and social breakdown. The policy that sought to improve the lives of the poorest has succeeded merely in the more efficient management of poverty; the concentration of mass unemployment and deprivation in one place, regulated, but unrelieved, creates an intensification of the ills it was supposed to remedy.

This is made all the more obvious by the adjacent district of Torre Angela, built piecemeal and illegally in the 1950s and 1960s by the self-made on open countryside. It has grown more prosperous over time, but the area still creates an impression of improvisation, unlike the grandiose design of Bella Monaca. In Torre Angela, there are no footpaths, the houses are irregularly spaced, with here and there an ancient reminder of the rural past—sheep on a piece of waste ground, a shack with peeling door and overgrown with weeds. The people here who have bettered themselves look with resentment at their neighbours in Bella Monaca: we did it for ourselves, why can't they?—the implacability of the self-made against the unreconstructed.

The most obvious feature of Bella Monaca is shared with all those who live off the fag-end of the market economy in the West—the imitative gestures towards the life of the rich. Their clothes are stamped with false brand-names—Lacoste, Gucci, Nike—or they bear exotic emblems—Disneyland, University of California, the New York Giants; the cheap ear-ornaments, silvery rings on every finger, shiny hair-bows, lurex threads, sequined blouses are the tribute they pay to those who can afford the real thing. Their imitation of the styles of the wealthy show to what degree they live in a culture of dependent exclusion.

The estate dates only from the early eighties, a population of young couples, children and adolescents; all ties with the past have been broken, and the only common experience is that of the images and advertisements on televison and the desolation of Bella Monaca. Drugs are the most destructive influence here; there are two bars where the *spacciatori* (dealers) work; they offer free samples to the young people who sell for them, and they are soon hooked. The drug culture is propagated by contagion and conversion—a mixture of plague and religion, according to Antonello Stefanini, who works in a drugs advisory unit. When I asked him what permits such an easy passage to drugs in rich Western society, he said 'What is there to stop them? Where would the resistance come from, where are the alternative moral values?' Drugs, he says, have replaced religion in the consumer societies as 'the heart of a heartless world'. The horror-stories certainly confirm the heartlessness: the girl of fourteen who came home from school to find her mother dead in the bath—both sons had been dealing in drugs and bringing home expensive presents which she knew could have only one source; the mother desperately trying to contain her son's dependency, going from house to house begging for the money to supply his daily needs. She has sold everything to prevent him from turning to crime; her attempts at concealment are vain, and the desperation of her efforts make her the object of great pity to neighbours who can do nothing for her. One young woman recently threw herself out of a window in her despair at not being able to find the money for her fix.

In spite of the cruelty and violence, it is wrong to think of the people simply as victims. Umberto Castra teaches skills to fifteen young people from severely deprived families. He insists that the people of Bella Monaca contribute significantly to the economy of Rome, even though largely to the unofficial economy. Between five and seven-thirty in the morning is the time to be here; the buses into the city are full, especially women and young people, many of the latter under fourteen. They are doing domestic work, labouring, bar work, waiting, selling; one boy is selling single roses in plastic tubes to motorists in traffic jams, another contraband cigarettes; those who have nothing else to sell—many of them little more than children—sell their bodies.

It is mostly women who bear the excruciating costs of social despair. It is difficult to say which one was suffering more—the woman who dare not go out because she is afraid of the nameless terrors of the neighbour-hood, or the woman whose husband's overwhelming jealousy will not let her out of his sight.

At six o'clock in the evening, Salvatore is waiting for his wife to come home. The flat is a cheerless place: bare tiled-floor, a big cupboard of red-dish marbled plastic, three children watching the black and white television set, absorbing blankly its exhortations to a life of leisure and liberal spending. Salvatore's wife has gone to do domestic work at Torre Angela. Yesterday, the employers kept her for eleven hours, although they are paying her for four hours daily. When she protested, she was told she could go if she was not satisfied—there are plenty more who would welcome the job.

Along the walkways, we meet a television crew: the cameras they carry are probably the most expensive objects ever seen at Bella Monaca. They are making a documentary. However sympathetic the programme makers are—and these are—their function is other than that which they imagine. The poor are invisible in this rich city; by bringing their pain to the screen, by parading their injuries and humiliations, they keep alive in the viewers a sense of the horror of poverty, lengthen the distance between the comfortable majority and those whose privations appear both repelling and incomprehensible.

The blocks are called *residenze*; this has been shortened to R1, R2, so that when people give their address, this is reduced to a letter and a number. In the open space behind the highest towers, cypress trees have been planted, graveyard trees. The people say this is fitting, for it is *il cimitero dei viventi*—the cemetery of the living.

Gino Pogliazicci came off drugs just a year ago. He sees nothing wrong with being both a committed Catholic and a Communist, to save lives in this life and souls in the next. Gino's father was a partisan in the Second World War, and afterwards was reduced to catching songbirds with a net and selling them for food to the people living in the shanties around what is now Cinecitta. His mother died when he was two, and his father three years later, and Gino was brought up by a friend of his mother's. They were very poor, and lived on minestrone and bread for every meal, every day. He felt angry and hurt that his parents had been taken away from him; while still a child, he started stealing, at first only food and small sums of money, but later he went house-breaking. He has been in prison twelve times; later, he became a drug addict, sleeping in the streets and stealing routinely to feed the habit. You would never think so to see him now; he works voluntarily with addicts, and is a social worker with the church. A warm and generous man who knows everyone in the bleak suburb of Centocelle where he lives, I asked him how he had managed to come off drugs when he was in his mid-thirties. He said 'Do you believe in miracles?' While he was being detoxified, his brother died of AIDS: he had used an infected needle to inject heroin. He has left a widow and two children.

Gino works as maintenance engineer in a block of flats that were originally constructed for private occupation, at a daily rent of 80,000 lire (about £30). Before they were completed, they were invaded and taken over by homeless people; all two hundred and fifty flats were immediately squatted. The municipal authorities have agreed to pay the company rent for four years, and to compensate for any damage caused. The flats are small, intended as a luxury *pied-à-terre*; ceramic floors, wide windows, modern fittings, marble and tiles. Although it was despair that led to the take-over, the flats are unsuitable for families. Potenza is a sad-faced woman of about forty, who lives with her daughter, eighteen, and handicapped son who is seventeen. She was abandoned by her husband when the boy was a baby; he fell into a coma that lasted several months, and when it was discovered that he was brain-damaged, his father departed. Potenza has lived with relatives and friends, always moving on when the patience of those who sheltered them was exhausted. Potenza has to sleep in the same bed as her son. He goes to a special school, but at weekends and in the holidays, there is no relief for his mother. The daughter, Romina, has just left school, and is engaged. There is no work in the area. Potenza tells her to get a skill so if she finds herself in the same position as her mother, she won't be dependent on charity. Romina listens; a young woman with wide green eyes and fair hair. It is clear that she doesn't believe such things could ever happen to her; a faint smile and a look of serene self-containment indicate that she thinks her life will be different.

Beneath Potenza lives Celeste ('Celeste Aida', she says with a smile.) She is a waif-like young woman in her early twenties, dark eyes, thin face and a nimbus of black hair. Her four-year-old son, Moreno, has been removed from her care by social workers, because the man she is living with is on drugs. Celeste picks up a picture of the child, wipes the dust from it with her cuff. He is being looked after by the nuns; all his toys are set out on shelves in the flat, waiting for his return. She doesn't like living here, at Val Cannuta, but at least it's better than the streets. All it needs is for her boy-friend to come off drugs, and then they'll give Moreno back to her. The truth is that her boy-friend is not easily going to give up drugs; she is refusing to face up to the choice which she has already made. On the dressing-table there is a large picture of Marilyn Monroe, and, in a silver-gilt frame, a Virgin and Child. Many of the flats contain transnational culture—sports heroes, pop stars, Maradona or Madonna; beneath a picture of Michael Jackson, a young woman has written '*Michael, tu sei mia vita.*' You are my life.

Linda is in her sixties, a big woman with iron-grey hair, who has a bad
heart and can walk only with great difficulty. She started work when she
was ten, cutting the wheat in other people's fields. Gino has brought her
a parcel of food—some pasta, eggs, oil, tinned tomatoes and fruit. It is
not for her, but for the family of her son who is dying of drugs. His body
is ruined, his liver, kidneys, there is no hope for him. Tears of anger and
grief stand in her eyes. '*E un macello*,' she keeps saying, '*un vero macello*';
it's a ruin, her life and her son's are both wrecked. Linda and her husband
used to be *portieri* at a block of flats in Ostia, but were thrown out, literally
onto the street when the new owner wanted to modernize it. They occupied
the council offices in protest, and came to Val Cannuta when they heard
of the organized squatting.

Poverty is changed, people tell you everywhere, but people are still poor.
How, then, was poverty different in the past? Alfonso is in his sixties; he
grew up in a village in Umbria, where his family owned some poor land
that had to be hoed by hand, where they grew grapes, olives and vegetables
for their own consumption; there were a few pigs and sheep. Alfonso's
mother had twelve children, of whom two died in infancy, and she had
almost as many abortions. His parents were always up by five thirty in the
morning, working in the fields, and his mother had to fetch the day's supply
of water from the well. When the father died, the land was shared between
the sons, and there was not enough for them all to make a living. Alfonso
came to Rome and found work in service with a well-to-do family, where
he had to stand at attention like a soldier behind the table. He says his
employer taught him the secret of getting rich, and that is by living poor;
never eat more than a piece of cheese, an apple and some pasta, never
more than one glass of wine. 'As children', he says, 'we never saw money;
now children never see anything else.'

Alfonso's daughters are in service industries—one at hostess-school,
the other learning languages to become a tourist-guide. But few Italians
now want to work as domestic servants, a role filled in recent years by
Filipinos, Ethiopians and Sri Lankans.

Regino is in his thirties. He came to Rome, illegally, eight years ago,
and after two or three domestic jobs, he found himself working for the
family of one of the heads of the *Carabinieri* (the élite police force). 'When
I told him my papers weren't in order, he soon put things right.' Regino

grew up in the poor northernmost region of the Philippines, where his father worked as a labourer on other people's farms. Regino gained a scholarship, and he went on to do a degree in English:

> When I first came to Rome, the family I worked for didn't believe I was a teacher; they gave me inferior food and made me eat separately. Filipinos make good servants. We learn fast. We are discreet. Having known Spanish and American imperialism, we know how to adapt. I like it here. I send money home to my wife and three children, but I enjoy the materially better life. I don't know when I'll go back, or even if I will.

Regino's friend, Ali, is less happy here. He left Bangladesh when Ershad came to power; active in the Awami League, he came away to avoid political oppression. He hates exile, and has recently spent three months in hospital, recovering from the effects of drink. Many who come to Italy speak bitterly of having to learn alien tasks; the humiliation of having to work below their intellectual capacity, learning Italian cooking, mastering the skill of sweeping and cleaning to the Signora's satisfaction, waiting patiently while their dinner parties are prolonged into the early hours, and listening to their drunken indiscretions and racism without reacting.

Most domestic servants have a day off on Sundays; they go to the piazza in front of Termini Station or to Piazza Risorgimento near the Vatican walls. Karuna, Neville, Anura and Abey are from Sri Lanka, working for a property dealer, a factory owner, a lawyer and an astrologer, respectively. In Colombo, their jobs had been in a cigarette factory, the wholesale fruit market, government service. Abey says he works at the *pianoforte*—he means standing at the sink, washing and rinsing dishes. He doesn't want to stay in Europe, or become like Europeans.

> I don't want a car, I don't want more than one set of clothes or more food than I can eat. I don't want to go to discos or get drunk. I wouldn't be here if I could live in peace in Sri Lanka. The police are always on the lookout for terrorists. If somebody doesn't like you, he only has to denounce you, say you're a member of the JVP, (the guerrilla movement). They'll pick you up, and to make you talk, they'll beat you up, take out your fingernails. I don't want to go through all that

again. The worst thing about being here is that people underestimate you. If you don't speak Italian, they think it's because you are stupid.

Ali Hussein is one of the many Ethiopians who have sought refuge in Italy in the eighties. He was a university lecturer in Addis Ababa, but when the *Dergue* (the Marxist régime) came to power in 1974, the teachers were directed to go into the countryside to instruct the peasants in the meaning of the revolution. When this was unsuccessful, the teachers were accused of spreading anti-government propaganda. Ali fled to Somalia, and taught history in a school in Mogadishu. Later, he went on to Saudi Arabia, working as a clerk in the office of an oil company. He came to Rome on a tourist visa. He is more free than he has ever been, but also poorer; here, he has worked as a domestic, as a gardener, as a driver, and as a vendor, selling cigarette lighters in the Metro. He now lives in a monastery, and eats at the *mensa sociale* run by Caritas (the world-wide Catholic Charity). His whole life experience has been one of steadily lowered status and greater insecurity. He is waiting to go to Canada, but all the time he knows that regulations are being tightened in all the traditional countries of asylum. In the mornings, Ali Hussein teaches English voluntarily at the Caritas reception centre for foreigners.

Among those in his class are a number of Poles, who have sought refuge in Italy during the time of the present Pope. Some of these people have been learning another kind of lesson in economics, quite different from the sombre instruction they had received at home. The deep penetration of Western life by monetary values is a harsh reality, against which the most indissoluble solidarities, like the most fervent piety, are equally unavailing. When Marie first came to Rome, she was so overwhelmed by the abundance of things that she spent her day off taking pictures of the shop windows and sending them to her mother in Warsaw; now she has discovered that having money with no goods to spend it on is not necessarily a more painful experience than being tantalized by teeming goods and no means of acquiring them. Many Poles are working as casual labourers, cleaning cars at the traffic lights, selling on the streets, activities that suggest the Third World city rather than a European capital.

Those people who are in Italy illegally submit to conditions and work that are degrading. Noury is from Morocco; he sells lighters on the street.

He was studying in France, but dropped out after a year, and was not allowed to return. There are eight children in his family, so he has come to Rome to make some money. He was living in a shared room in a *pensione* in the winter, but was turned out when the tourist season started. He now sleeps in a car which he shares with a friend, for a 'rent' of 18,000 lire a night (about £7.50). The car doesn't work, but it provides shelter from the worst of a damp Rome spring. Two brothers from Algeria are working in a restaurant; they must work every day of the year, from nine till three, and then from six till midnight or later. Between them, they earn 300,000 lire a month—about £120. They live in one room, but if they complain, they are under threat of deportation if their status is disclosed; they are virtually captive.

The most conspicuous of the people from the Third World are the petty vendors, called familiarly the *Vuo' Comprar*—'Please buy'; with their bulky shoulder-bags of merchandise, leather goods, belts, handbags, sunglasses, cheap jewellery, novelties, which they buy from dealers and sell on the streets. Saow is from Senegal; now thirty-three, he went to Paris to look for work when his father died, entering illegally through Marseille. After a month, he was picked up by the police, handcuffed, gaoled and deported to Dakar. He says 'The French come to Dakar, none of them are poor, so what are they doing in my country if not making money there? But they don't want us doing the same thing in Paris.' He came to Rome because, as many people admit, it is easier and the police are less thorough. Saow is selling sunglasses; he lives in a rundown apartment on Via Casilina, which he shares with eleven other men, four in each of the three rooms. It is a bare, functional place, tiled floors, peeling walls, strip lighting on the flaking ceiling; a battered suitcase under the metal bed-frame, a suit under polythene. Saow eats take-away pizza twice a day. In Dakar, he worked in a shoe-factory, and later, as a shoe-repairer. He has three children, who live with their mother and grandmother. He doesn't care if his stay in Rome doesn't last, as long as it provides him with just enough money to start his own workshop in Dakar.

Sitting as he does by the side of the road, Saow cannot fail to be aware of the attitudes of the people; many are hostile, some deliberately trample the merchandise as they pass. Many are openly racist. He doesn't speak much Italian, but says that the language of contempt doesn't require words.

Among the poorest in Rome, and the focus of a disproportionate resentment in view of their numbers (two or three thousand), have been the
gypsies, especially the Khorikhanè, the Muslim nomads from Yugoslavia.
Attempts by the municipality to provide camp sites with basic amenities
have sometimes led to ugly incidents—demonstrations by the residents
of working-class areas, many of them Communist Party supporters.

On the northern periphery, at Monte Sacro, there is a small piece of
ground with fifteen or twenty caravans, and a few sheds, improvised structures of plywood, polythene and perspex, housing no more than a hundred
people. The site is a wasteland, reached by a muddy path bordered with
trees and fragrant in spring with the lilac flowers of wistaria. In front of
the open space there is an auto repair shop and two blocks of flats. This
group of families moved here four months ago: the land was discovered
by the workers of Opera Nomadi, a small organization set up by volunteers
to help integrate the gypsies into the life of the city. The people arrived
by night. 'If we had come in the daytime', says Ekrem, 'the people who
live here would have thrown us out. We had to move quietly, so as not to
disturb them. When they woke up in the morning and found us more or
less established, they were more inclined to accept us.' The land belongs
to the municipality, so they are dealing with public authorities and not
private owners.

The caravans—mostly small and rounded, dating from the 1950s—the
battered cars and ancient snub-nosed lorries, are parked around a central
open space. On sunny spring days, most of the furniture is out of doors—a
big leatherette sofa in front of the caravan, mats and folding metal chairs,
wooden stools; clothes hang from improvised washing lines or are thrown
over the bushes to dry. Fires are burning, and a chicken or rabbit is cooking
in a pan over a trivet. One woman is sorting through a box of mushroom
stalks discarded from a hotel; another is separating mouldy oranges from
those that are still edible. The spent ash from earlier fires is whipped by
the wind into eddies of grey dust.

Ekrem is in his late thirties. He has seven children, and came from
Yugoslavia twenty years ago. He left, he says, because he didn't want to
die of hunger. Ekrem buys copper scrap from factories, and works the
materials into utensils, pans and ornaments by beating it. It is the custom
for the women to get money by begging, *l'elemosina*, 'alms' as they call it.

Ekrem finds it incomprehensible that the rich should resent giving to those who have nothing. 'God made us poor and them rich, but God made us all. That's what they tell you, but they don't act as if they believed it. When we ask them for help, they spit on us and call us *stronzo* ('shithead'). Ekrem's eldest daughter, Yagoda, is sixteen, pale face, dark eyes, long red dress. She doesn't go to school: there is too much work to be done, looking after the younger children, while her mother is away from the camp.

Mustafa is in his sixties. He lives alone in his small caravan: inside, a mattress and a tapestry picture of the mosque at Sarajevo. In front of the van he has made a little garden, some fennel and basil in pots. Mustafa makes model antique pistols, of carved wood and beaten metal. From Bosnia-Herzogovina, he speaks a mixture of Romany, Italian and Serbo-Croat. As he tells his story, he acts it out. He puts on an old bowler hat and squats beside the caravan, then gets up and mimes working at the manufacture of pots and pans, indicating that this is how his family lived for hundreds of years. He repeats the performance a number of times to suggest continuity. Then, suddenly, in 1941 . . . He closes the caravan door, and struts up to it in the way of soldiers. He knocks heavily on the door. It is four o'clock in the morning. All the family are sleeping. They wake up in confusion. They are ordered outside. He mimes the act of kissing his mother goodbye—making her face with his hand, he kisses his thumb and forefinger as tenderly as though he were kissing her lips. He, as a boy of thirteen, slips away. The men, women and young children were all taken away and shot by Croatian fascists; he mimes the gunning down, and the kicking of the bodies into a rough ditch. Mustafa himself ran away and joined the partisans. As he acts out the great sorrow that has marked him, tears form in his eyes; one eye is permanently closed, from when he was captured and tortured by the Fascists. After the war, he had no one left in Yugoslavia; he attached himself to this group of Khorikhanè, who have become his family, and has been travelling with them ever since. Mustafa say that his father was a Muslim and his mother a Catholic, so he is half and half. We are all children of God, he says; it is only when people forget that that they start killing each other.

As Mustafa performs his story, a stillness falls over the yard. The young people pause and watch. Some smile; the woman peeling vegetables remains with her knife poised, the women stirring the pots freeze, spoon in hand. Even the men, leaning against the caravans, forget the cigarette in their mouth so that it almost scorches their lips. They have heard it all before, but they recognize the importance of reiteration. Alessandro is sixteen; he looks on, solemn and attentive. Mustafa is sometimes confused, even a little crazed; perhaps confusion is a refuge for the pain that has pursued him all these years. Perhaps, says Ekrem, he, too, has killed people. To think, he continues, we came from India two thousand years ago, and no one had harmed us before this.

Luigi Leonori runs the Caritas hostel for foreigners near Termini Station; one of the few organizations that provide beds, although only on a short-term basis, for the destitute. 'At first', he says, 'the people from the Third World were seen as rather picturesque. It added something to the charm of the city. Now people are saying "What are all these foreigners doing here?" and secondly, "If they have nothing, it is their own fault."' Rome has been one of the last major European capitals to have experienced the presence of people from the South. Here, as elsewhere, it has a profoundly conscientizing influence on the people. The refugees, migrants and incomers are, as it were, the involuntary ambassadors from the majority of the earth's people who are, overwhelmingly, poor and Black. Their effect is to make the Europeans aware of how menaced and unsustainable their prosperity may be.

Late on Sunday evening, the servants are separating after their day out, and going their different ways. The best clothes are crumpled as they linger in the twilight, a can of Coke and slice of pizza in hand. As they get onto the bus, they take off the gold chains and medallions they have been wearing and place them in wallet and handbag, so as not to attract the attention of thieves. Their bodies slump forward in the uncomfortable bus seat. The day of sharing and laughter and speaking the familiar language is over for another week. Their own reflection stares back, bleak and smudged, from the darkening window.

11/MARKETING THE WILDERNESS

I F ROVANIEMI IN FINNISH LAPLAND looks like a frontier town, this is not only because the city was ninety-six per cent destroyed as the Germans retreated in 1944, and had to be totally reconstructed, but also because it marks a less tangible frontier; it is the site of economic transformation, from an agrarian society of reindeer farmers and timber growers into a service economy of administration and tourism.

With a population of 30,000, Rovaniemi is just south of the Arctic circle, at the edge of what is, perhaps mistakenly, seen as the last wilderness of Europe. It also has the distinction of being the home town of Santa Claus; when Concorde is seen on the world's television screens every December, laden with gifts for deprived children, this spectacular event takes place at the airport here. There is a Father Christmas village, extensive log restaurants with blazing fires and the pelts of dead bears spread-eagled across the chimney-breast. Ski-slopes have been carved into the hillsides, great stony wounds in summer, with its brief—one hundred days—growing season. Northern Finland is now marketing its most remarkable feature—its extraordinary landscape.

In September comes the *ruska*, the colouring of the trees. It starts with the groundcover, the bushes of sweet Arctic berries, ptarmigan berries and overripe bilberries, turning them shades of crimson and maroon; then the aspen and mountain-ash trees, and finally, the birches, change to colours that vary from blood-red to spectral yellow, vibrant against the sombre pines. The first needles of ice form on still mountain lakes, and trees that have withstood two hundred years of Arctic winds finally fall, and lie, bleached as bone in the scree.

Although tourists, perhaps jaded by the polluted beaches and packaged pleasures of Southern Europe, are coming in increasing numbers, unemployment in Finnish Lapland remains at about twenty per cent. The shift into an urbanized and service economy is not without pain. As recently as 1965, a majority of the people of Finland still remained country-dwellers.

On Toripuistikko, one of the main streets, there is a hotel and college combined, where young people are being trained by the catering industry. Maarit Puirava is a round-faced young woman of nineteen, with clear eyes and wide smile, who is training to be a cook. She comes from a small town, 250 kilometres to the south, to join the three hundred students who will go from here to serve in hotels and restaurants all over the country. Maarit's father drives a tractor, and her mother is a child-minder. Formerly, they were farmers, but as their village grew, it became more difficult to take the cows across the asphalt road to pasture, so they sold the land for development. Maarit will go to Helsinki, but she dreams of going home one day to the little town, and opening a first-class restaurant there.

Arto Kuukkeli is from Sodankyla, 130 kilometres north of Rovaniemi. His father is a cable-layer, his mother a shop-assistant. They went from reindeer farming into regular employment because it had become uneconomic without another job to supplement their income. Arto is learning to be a waiter. Like Maarit's course, his also takes two years. There is, they complain, a great deal of theory. Maarit must learn nutrition, must do chemistry and physics, diet and biology, and they both learn culinary English, French and Swedish; while Arto has lessons in carrying dishes and glasses, and in bar work, including the making of such mythic drinks as 'reindeer tears'. He also has to do maths, because restaurants are increasingly dispensing with cashiers. We also have lessons in psychology, he says proudly: they must learn to keep their temper and anticipate the needs of customers. He has no difficulty, because he is by nature a patient young man, pale and upright in his white shirt, black tie and trousers. Such a life must appear very tempting to the children of reindeer herders; and yet Arto also wants to return to Sodankyla, where he dreams of opening a restaurant by day that would turn into a disco at night for the young. Most young people do not willingly leave even what some cynically refer to as the smallest 'one-reindeer towns'. If Maarit and Arto had stayed at home, their life would have been like that of many of their contemporaries—hanging round the farms, waiting for a few days' seasonal work here and there. Under-employment and boredom have led to a serious drink problem among the young. Maarit even knows of one or two who have committed suicide.

The charm and youth of Arto and Maarit can only add to the agreeable experiences waiting to be marketed here. For one thing, the sun remains above the horizon from the sixth of June until the eighth of July; the *ruska* in September is one of the most exhilarating sights in the world; and in March and April, when the light returns, the snow is unspoilt and the clear Arctic air dazzling. Even in December, the darkness is attenuated by the whiteness of the landscape; and when the spring comes, the trees are green within a few days. Spring marches northwards at the rate of six kilometres a day.

Kyosti Urponen is professor of Sociology in the new University of Lapland; a keen monitor of the change in sensibility that comes about with the shift to the service economy:

> Urban people have a split response to nature. During the week, they are exploiting nature, standing above it, making it serve them. Then at the weekend, they seek leisure in it, look for spiritual values and escape. This is a contradiction; what you abuse in your daily life cannot console you in your free time. Those who still live in the country have a different attitude; the farmer, the reindeer-keeper still remain within nature, and they have respect and honour towards it. They know nature can be a threat, snow, gales and mists. But because they live within it, they neither abuse it nor romanticize it.

There has always been tourism in Lapland. Traditionally, this meant hiking, which requires minimal infrastructure; in fact, all you need is a pair of legs, some warm clothes and a certain amount of stamina. The hiking centres were modest places—a cabin for those who got lost, or were overtaken by night or sudden mist. Now there are elaborate hotels and lodges, so self-contained that the landscape becomes nothing more than a highly decorative background to some other activity—tennis, squash, Turkish baths. The countryside becomes a backdrop, and people are even more estranged from it. Kyosti Urponen: 'The people who used to go hiking were peasant and working-class people. Now the well-to-do have come to show them how it should be done. And of course, the big companies from the south have their own cabins, luxurious retreats in the wilderness, a perk for employees.' These cabins are built on rocky promontories and dominate the landscape—one belongs to a pharmaceutical company, one to a television station, another to an oil refinery. All are constructed from the wood of fallen pines; when the trees die, they do not decay because of the low level of bacterial activity in the cold air, and because of the tar which is a natural preservative of the wood.

The impact of tourism is not all negative. By concentrating facilities in a few areas, the damage to the environment can be localized. It also employs many people. There is a tendency, as in many major industries, towards sub-contracting; small family concerns give work to up to half a dozen people—handicrafts and pottery businesses are supported by hotels and restaurants. But tourism does depend on a buoyant economy; at the first hint of recession, it is the first industry to suffer.

Kyosti Urponen insists that there is nothing wrong with tourism: it is simply the way that it is promoted. People are not enriched by understanding and knowledge of the world they visit, but their prejudices are packaged with the trip.

And there is so much to learn, to be read in the landscape. In the 1930s, the climate was about two degrees warmer than it is now, so they were very optimistic about the forests regenerating if they were cut down. Seeds and plants from further south were introduced, but they simply died. Now reforestation is carried out with seeds and plants from within Lapland; varieties from more than 200 kilometres away are banned. It has been discovered that seventy kilometres is a crucial distance. Because the limit of the forest growth around here is 500 metres above sea level, no trees above 300 metres can be chopped down; no one knows how they will regenerate. The reason why each tree is a slightly different shade of yellow or red is that each tree is an individual, and it depends upon the genetic code of each one. The *ruska* comes every year at almost exactly the same date. Daylight is the only invariant which determines why you can predict it exactly—around the seventeenth of September. People think it is the frost; but there are frequently frosts in August, yet the leaves don't change colour then. The colour-change comes from the ground up—the small juolukka plants react to the cooling air by sugar-production, and this is what turns them vivid red.

But if tourists are indifferent to the landscape, their effect upon the Lapps, the original inhabitants of Northern Finland, has been even more damaging. The indigenous people should be called the Sami, according to Nils-Aslak Valkeapaa. His book, *Greetings from Lapland, the Sami— Europe's Forgotten People*, is a bitter protest against the Finnish (and, indeed, Soviet, Norwegian and Swedish) colonists who have devalued and dominated the Lapps, and then, not having quite succeeded in destroying the culture, have turned their living-places into museums. Of the tourist, Valkeapaa says 'Drives a car. Fast. Curses the mosquitoes in summer and the snow in winter. Enjoys the company of his whisky bottle. Is discontented. Imagines everyone is there just to wait on him. Believes he is doing the people in the place a favour.'

In the forest, one hundred kilometres north of Rovaniemi, there is a replica, authentic to the last detail, of a Lappish village; tents of birch-bark and moss, packed against a frame of birch branches, about eight feet high at its apex. In each tent, there are logs to sit on, the embers of a fire, some tea-kettles and toasting forks. In a clearing between the tents a big fire smoulders. A party of Finnish people park their Nissan Bluebird at the edge of the forest, and bring their provisions to the fire. They boil some water, cook sausages—impaled four at a time on the toasting fork—open up their packets of cheese, rye bread and cartons of orange juice. They turn up their collars against the raw wind, blow on their fingers.

The Lapps in Finland number about three thousand now. If the people of northern Finland are entering the service economy, it is the Lapps who have been the real victims. Most ceased to be nomads in the 1930s, by which time they had been driven to a few areas in the far north. Most have motorized sledges now, but at one time they might have walked up to one hundred kilometres a day. They are a small ethnic minority, and a very exotic one. As such, they have received much attention from researchers and anthropologists. As Nils-Aslak Valkeapaa says:

They entered the money economy through capitalization of production; one motor-sledge was worth about thirty reindeer, so the small herders soon lost theirs, and had to go and work for the big reindeer-keepers. Because of the advantages of technical equipment, there was a surplus of people not required for work. With unemployment, the social state makes its appearance in the Lappish economy. A Lapp was originally valued insofar as he was a good reindeer-keeper and dog-trainer; then he was valued to the extent that he could mend and maintain a motor-sledge; and now a person is valued insofar as he is a good bookkeeper who knows where to send the application forms for grants and social benefits. You can trace this development through the drawings of Lappish children. Originally, their pictures were of the sun, mountains, reindeer, father slinging the lasso; that gave way to drawings of motor-sledges covered with badges of Shell and Mobil.

The Lapps had no private ownership of land. They moved with their reindeer herds, from winter to summer camp. As the Finns pushed further north, the Lapps retreated. There is nowhere now where the Lapps constitute more than fifty per cent of the population. Salmon fishing, on which some groups depended, is now subject to fishing permits from the government. And incomers build cabins and claim ownership of the adjacent water. To the Lapps that makes no sense. They used to build fences around the camp, but only to protect the reindeer, but nobody owned it, in a capitalist sense. It wasn't mortgaged.

It was a shamanic culture, although Christianized from early in the Middle Ages. The Christian priests adapted the religion to the customs and celebrations of the Lappish people. There is a story of a famous shaman call Akmeli. Whenever he went into a trance, his wife alone knew the formulaic incantation that would rouse him from it. One day when he was in a deep trance, she forgot the words that were the sole way of bringing him back to consciousness. She tried and tried to remember, but failed. The shaman lay there, inert, as if dead. In the end, to the great grief of the whole community, he was buried. Many years later, the wife suddenly remembered the words. She spoke them; and as she did, the skeleton of her long buried husband rose up from the grave.

Reijo Sarvola is seventy-six, now retired, a former inspector of social welfare in the district. To reach his cabin requires a five kilometre walk across a ravine, over the cracked green quartzite face of the fells. The cloud is low, so that it seems the tops of the hills—which are the stems of what were far higher mountains, crushed by glaciers that retreated from this area only ten thousand years ago—are shadowed by mist; and with the birches the colour of flame, it seems as if the hills are burning. The silence is broken only by a silver thread of water falling into a placid lake— formerly a holy place of the Lapps, later the site of Christian baptisms. The water from the lake, drunk from a pinewood bowl, tastes of an icy absence of chemicals. The chubby and friendly kukkele bird follows walkers from tree to tree. At intervals, there are lodges, where you can make tea and light a fire, stay overnight if you are stranded. Most people have a story of having been caught by sudden fog; of pausing to throw a stone where they would have walked; and of hearing it echo from the ravine a few seconds later.

Reijo Sarvola's cabin is a tiny hut of pine, nine feet by nine. It contains two bunks, a small table, wooden stumps for chairs, a stove built by Reijo. The wood fire gives out a fierce resinous heat. There is salmon and oatmeal bread, and a serving of cloudberries, tart, corn-coloured, said to be richer in vitamin C than any other fruit.

Here, we are at the very edge of the tree-line. The pines that face the wind have broken and snapped, but have regenerated, contorted but tenacious. The trees that grow behind them are upright and regularly shaped. There are fourteen words in Lappish to describe pines, each one indicating a certain stage of growth or decay of the tree. At ground level, there is a covering of miniature bluish juniper trees, which lie all winter, buried and preserved beneath the snow-level, which here is seventy centimetres. Beneath the fallen grey shaft of a pine lie the remains of a reindeer, bones, hooves and yellowing skull in the position where they were trapped by the falling tree.

After Soviet atomic tests in the 1970s, the lichen—a sage-green, slow-growing variety—was so badly affected by fall-out, that it was predicted that this would mean the end of reindeer-farming in Finnish Lapland, because this lichen was the primary food of the reindeer. Yet the following summer brought an abundance of a particular kind of Arctic moth: the caterpillars feed on birch leaves, which that year they ate in vast quantities. The droppings from these caterpillars made the ground very fertile, and this permitted the diminutive grasses that generally grow between the lichen to reach unusual heights; with the result that as the reindeer ate, they consumed only this hay, and were preserved from eating the contaminated lichen. This story is told as a kind of parable about Finland's relations with the Soviet Union; a series of miraculous escapes.

In the warmth of the cabin, Reijo remembers conditions in the area when he came here immediately after the Second World War. The whole of Rovaniemi had been evacuated before it was systematically destroyed. There was nothing left:

> The first thing the Finns will build is a sauna, and that is what happened then. One day, I was in a jeep with an official from one of the international aid agencies who was on a fact-finding mission. We saw this family who had just come from the sauna, father, mother, several children, picking their way through the snow. They were completely naked. The official was appalled to see such poverty. I said to him, 'That is a typical family, just coming back from work in the fields.' The aid flowed in. In a parcel of clothing that came from America, there was a dress suit in perfect condition. It was given to a peasant, who I subsequently saw behind a handplough, with the tails of this coat flapping behind him.

The selling of these unique landscapes as a retreat for weary Europeans tired of urban life leads to epochal changes in the Finnish economy. Whether the passage of the children of reindeer-farmers into the service economy is any more liberating for them than it is for the children of former workers in mine and mill in Britain, who are treading the same path, is a question that has yet to be confronted.

12 / THE APOTHEOSIS
OF THE MARKET ECONOMY: McLEAN COUNTY

M CLEAN COUNTY, IN CENTRAL ILLINOIS, is one of the richest
agricultural areas of the United States, and in this prosperous
region, the freedoms that are available to those where the market system
is least contested have reached their highest point of refinement and elaboration.

Bloomington-Normal are twin cities in the midle of McLean County.
Their combined population is about one hundred thousand, and they
represent the kind of community in which the majority of Americans
live. Perhaps here, the contradictions of the market economy have been
resolved.

Downtown Bloomington, like many city centres in the United States,
looks as if it has been abandoned. Many of its stores are closed, and at
night, it is almost completely deserted, except for a few wraith-like
derelicts in empty doorways. On the sides of tall, flat-roofed buildings are
painted ancient advertisements for Jim Beam or Fresh-Baled Hay. Some
effort has been made to refurbish the area; lawyers seem to be its principal
daytime occupants. No building pre-dates 1900, when Bloomington was
destroyed by fire. Within two days, the city council had decided to rebuild
the court-house, an impressive centrepiece, now being turned into a
museum of local history. The most significant construction work downtown is a new 'correctional facility'—evidence that this prosperous place
is expanding rapidly, indeed, has taken on something of the excitements
and anxieties of a boom-town.

City centres, however, reveal little about the community. The real activity is on the periphery. There are the fast-food chains—Macdonald's,

announcing '70 billion sold'; the shopping malls with their 'anchor stores'; the retirement facility of Westminster Village (perhaps one of the reasons for the vigour of spoken American is that it has to battle against official euphemisms—'Wrinkle City' people call it); the over-ornamented chateau of Jumer's hotel, where the phone-booths are wooden confessionals and there is a Watteau-esque painting over the door of the boutique; the housing development at North Pointe eating up the cornland, where three-car garages are a built-in feature and instant landscaping occurs on the grand scale—acres of turf, a lake, a plantation of full-grown red maple.

Bloomington was originally a railway town, where the first Pullman car was built. The abandoned rail workshops are reminiscent of parts of formerly industrial Britain; but the city simply moved away from its industrial base, to the east and north, and is now indistinguishable from Normal. It was always split between the rough railroad workers on the one hand, and retired farmers on the other, in the elegant mansions of Franklin Square, where Adlai Stevenson's family lived. The city had a history of trade union militancy, and there was a celebrated red-light district, where Richard Pryor's grandmother kept a lively brothel.

There is little trace of such things now, where everything suggests prosperity and self-confidence. However, even this fortress of tradition is having to come to terms with the internationalizing of its economy, and the—for many—reluctant acknowledgement that the United States no longer enjoys the undisputed industrial supremacy which has long been taken for granted. While State Farm Insurance (which started here) remains the largest employer (six thousand workers), and the Illinois State University creates an agreeable sense of security, the Beich Candy factory has been taken over by Nestlé, and Funk's Seeds is now owned by Ciba-Geigy; while the Eureka vacuum-cleaner factory is controlled by a Swedish company. But the most dramatic symbol of change is the vast new Chrysler-Mitsubishi joint-venture plant, which sits in the cornfields like a gleaming ocean-going liner, stranded, out of its element, in the rich black earth of McLean County.

If there is anxiety about the power of Japan ('I'm sure glad I didn't know they'd be here when I was fighting them in World War Two'), and unease about drugs ('It's a Communist attempt to weaken the backbone of the next generation') and concern about America's alliances ('Why have the

Germans gone soft on defending themselves?'), this scarcely disturbs the traditional structure of the day—early work-start, early to bed—which was determined by patterns of farming life brought by German settlers in the mid-nineteenth century. The farmland here is so rich that in the humid summer nights they say, 'You can hear the corn grow.' McLean County is Republican, conservative and pious. Churches stand on almost every block, some of them newly built and testifying to a living faith—First Presbyterian, Mennonite, Seventh Day Adventist, Lutheran, Methodist, Baptists, The African Methodist Episcopal, Catholic. German inscriptions—*Friedenskirche*—remain on some foundation-stones. The German language was abruptly extinguished here in 1917, when the congregations of some churches were besieged, even attacked, by angry neighbours. The Mennonites, like many Germans, had come here because of their commitment to peace, and their flight from conscription in the Prussian army. It is significant that many of their descendants showed little sympathy with those who sought to avoid the Vietnam draft; the mutation from radical to conservative could be as swift in the mid-West as it was total.

Conservative values are, in any case, it turns out, extremely flexible. Most people insist that they are 'moderates' anyway; and they seldom appear upset if what they believe is glaringly at odds with what is actually happening in the United States. For instance, as part of their cherished beliefs, many cite 'the work ethic, prudence and thrift, love of country, local autonomy and family values'. Yet many of these are being eroded by existing—and apparently inexorable—patterns of economic development. The growth in personal indebtedness and consumer credit is scarcely compatible with the idea of one truly conservative farmer who said he didn't believe in credit cards, 'because if owning four hundred acres of good county soil doesn't prove I'm creditworthy, a whole acre of plastic won't change that'. Similarly, many expressed the conviction that the job of government should limit itself to 'removing garbage and taking care of the nation's defence'. Yet Bloomington offers rich pickings to lawyers with their inventive interpretation of a baroque structure of rules and regulations, both local and federal. (There has been a fifty-eight per cent increase in the number of lawyers in Illinois in the past decade, according to Tom Jacob.) At a recent lawyers' convention in Chicago, Jack Porter, also a lawyer, was shocked to hear one speaker declare that

'One should live one's whole life in the expectation that any episode in it may become the subject of litigation.' One of the talking points in town was a case from Florida, where a young woman was suing a former boy-friend for failing to show up at a High School prom he had promised to take her to. She was claiming that the investment in a new dress and hair-do had led to serious losses.

Family values, too, are not quite the unassailable refuge they may once have been. The very explosion of opportunities, the exigencies of the eco-nomy, scatter families across the continent with almost as divisive a force as that which sent so many migrants from Europe in the first place. Tom Jacob says: 'My father was one of fifteen, born between 1895 and 1920. They all grew up in a town of five thousand people. Of my generation, there isn't one remaining in that town. We meet mostly for funerals now. The younger generation doesn't understand family like I understand it.' Sally Rudolph works as a pharmacist, and although her children have also left town, she doesn't feel that the separation in any way weakens the family. 'We talk on the telephone every week. The family becomes more precious because it is spread out. It means that you enjoy reunions and vacations the more.'

There is little sense that there are any great social or political battles to be fought in Bloomington. Concern for the environment was quickened by the 1988 drought, there are those who declare it is a scandal that anyone in America should end the day hungry and homeless; but even the gener-ation who fought for civil rights in the sixties are no longer animated by the same passionate urgency. Oscar Weddell was the first Black in Bloomington ever to have worked on the shop-floor of what was then a washing-machine factory:

> Blacks could join the union, but they could only do menial jobs. When I came out of the War, I was a sweeper in the plant. One night, there was no operator on a crucial machine—without it, the whole plant would have had to close down. They asked me if I could do it. I did; and the next day, when I went to get my broom, they told me I was being transferred to the job permanently.

Oscar was on Guam during the Second World War, building the air-strip, and he was there when the plane took off that dropped the atomic bomb on Nagasaki. His grandfather had been a slave, and the name came from his owner, General Waddell, in the Army of the Confederacy. During the Civil War, Oscar's grandfather went underground and fought with the Union army. His uncle served in the Spanish-American war, his brother was in Europe in World War Two, his children fought in Vietnam. 'When young Blacks say to me "We ain't got no country", I say to them "I fought so that you should have. I'm a Black man, but I'm a Black American."'

John Goldrick, publisher of the Pantagraph newspaper ('fiscally and politically conservative, liberal on human and constitutional rights') is a vigorous proponent of American capitalism as a reflection of natural law. 'Why shouldn't you get on if you work hard, as opposed to someone who sits on his behind and does nothing?' John Goldrick fought in Korea, and saw Seoul ravaged: 'The only thing standing was Seoul cathedral. Now look at it. In thirty years, it has been transformed from Third World country to industrial power. There is no evidence, historically, that there are any limits to human desire, and that is what our way of life is built on.'

Many people express their dissatisfaction with liberal and conservative labels. 'Conservatism means doing old things in new ways; being innovative is not at odds with a love of tradition.' One man defined a conservative as 'someone who wants the government out of your wallet and into your bedroom; while a liberal wants the government out of your bedroom and into other people's wallets.'

The openness of people in the mid-West is very different from the tension in the big cities. Sometimes the friendliness seems a learned response, a public face, behind which more sober and calculated judgements are being made. However that may be, one of the most positive features of social life is the effort that goes into voluntary community work. Organized around the churches, support groups, the workplace, there is a vast reservoir of charitable and helping endeavour, from the Loaves and Fishes soup kitchen attached to the Art Deco bulk of Holy Trinity church, the SHARE (inter-denominational charity) cheap grocery scheme, which distributes around six hundred parcels a month in Bloomington, the Habitat house-building charity. Even the reconstructed village of New Salem, where Abraham Lincoln lived, near Springfield, is staffed by volunteers. The most significant force in this selflessness is the energy of the elderly; perhaps an acknowledgement that fewer of them are now among the poorest in the United States. Poverty has been feminized and made younger; single parents, children and low-income working families. Social security (old age pension) has remained politically inviolable, and many older people, recognizing their strength, are anxious to give back to society what they feel they have gained.

Although still overwhelmingly Republican, the expansion of the university and the changing economic structure mean that there is greater flexibility in the mid-West than once was the case; and the city still has its radicals and eccentrics. Ray Ryburn is described by some as 'the Thoreau of Bloomington'. In his seventies now, he wears denims, has a white beard, and is a lucid and engaging commentator on the United States. Of the sixty-five years of his working life, he had a regular job for barely ten of them:

> They talk of labour being adaptable now—well I've done everything, handled horses, worked on construction, peddled fruit on street corners. I agree with Gandhi, who said that he was not against machines as such, but against the idea that they saved labour; the labour they save is in the people starving on the streets. The time and energy saved are not given back to the people. Employers pay poor wages, and then get mad because they have to pay taxes to keep those who work for them at the level of subsistence. Pericles said 'The disgrace of poverty is not in the fact of being poor, but in declining the struggle against it.' I believe in capitalism, only if it doesn't have victims. Trouble is, all -isms have victims.

Ray Ryburn and his wife have raised eight children. He says they will spend a hundred dollars on one toy for a child, which is more than he ever spent on all of them together. 'If you want to keep up with the Joneses, just look at where the Joneses are heading.'

He believes that if the war machine is not replaced with suitable jobs, the people will never accept peace. 'It's easy to talk peace, but you must offer them something in place of war. People don't mind being told their faults—it's only when you try to correct them that they get mad. The only way is to show them how change would be in their best interests.' He says that equality before the law without social justice is no equality at all. Raised in the Pentecostal Church, he is no longer a churchgoer, but is still a believer. 'Being a Christian is like being a doctor, it's not in the profession but in the practice that it shows.'

Carol Reitan, who works for Community Action, is a Democrat, and the former mayor of Normal: her election showed that when it comes to local matters, there are no real differences between the parties. She is well aware of the social distinctions that operate in this ostensibly egalitarian society; nuances of precedence that mark out the subtleties of caste:

> Most of the old money came through the acquisition of land when it was sold cheaply. Old money is low-key and avoids ostentation. Its clothes are good but not showy. New money is less inhibited about display. Many people think there are no poor people here. They'll take part in 'Bread for the World' or 'Shoes for Poland' committees—they have a world consciousness, but not a local one. They have the good life, and they assume that anyone who doesn't isn't really trying. Poverty here is the poverty of things you cannot have, not a poverty of need.

Lawrence Irvin was administrative assistant to Adlai Stevenson during his period as Governor of Illinois. He lives in a house at the edge of Lake Bloomington, originally a summer cabin, but now a substantial structure. Lawrence is now nearly eighty. His house is full of mementoes of the Stevenson years. He takes down an autographed copy of the acceptance speech and nomination address given by Adlai Stevenson at the 1952 Democratic Convention. He asks me to read from it; as I do, his eyes fill with tears:

> Here, on the prairies of Illinois and the Middle West, we can see a long way in all directions. There are no barriers, no defences to ideas and aspirations. We want none; we want no shackles on the mind or spirit, no rigid patterns of thought, no iron conformity.

The sun bounces, a scarlet balloon, on a vast horizon; white-tailed deer appear among the pale grass of last summer. If the glaciers stopped at the terminal moraine which is now the site of McLean County, with its legacy of rich dark soil, it is easy to understand that people interpret this as a sign of the favour of Providence: in the stillness of early evening, you can even imagine you *see* the corn growing.

Diamond Star Motors

The furthest effects of market competition can be seen at Diamond Star Motors, a few miles from Bloomington; a joint venture between Chrysler and Mitsubishi, the plant is one of the most highly automated and robotized in the world. Ninety per cent of welding is done robotically, releasing the associates (the word 'worker' does not figure in the vocabulary) from dangerous and tedious operations. Almost half a billion dollars' worth of investment has gone into the 636-acre site in the midst of the green cornfields. This has produced just under three thousand jobs— about $175,000 per employee.

The works consists of a stamping shop, body shop, plastic moulding shop, paint shop and final assembly area; the conveyor lines are eight miles in total length. A one and a half mile track allows for the test-driving of every vehicle. The low white building is surrounded by a wire-mesh fence and rows of barbed wire—it resembles something between a military installation and a hospital facility.

Although this is an equal venture, few people in the plant can be unaware that Mitsubishi accounts for almost ten per cent of the formidable gross national product of Japan. One in ten of the Diamond Star workforce will be trained in Japan, for a period of up to thirty-seven weeks. There are about fifty Japanese employees at present, and 100–150 technical assistants on short-term visits to help production get under way. The plant opened in the autumn of 1988.

There are bound to be occasional frictions, cultural misunderstandings. Mitsubishi executives, who are required to work in Bloomington, are directed to come here. It's no good, as a senior executive explained, saying he has an ailing mother. If he fits the job, he comes. There have also been language difficulties, with the result that visual techniques have been substituted, where possible, for linguistic ones.

In spite of this, the Japanese say they have been surprised by the dedication of the Bloomington work-force. It is no accident that the site chosen is the Mid-West, where the work-ethic remains strong. The office hours of DSM are from 7.30 a.m. until 4.12 p.m. When the first three hundred jobs were advertised, there were more than thirty thousand applicants. You don't have to travel far in Bloomington before you meet disappointed

aspirants; and those accepted are the object of envy and admiration, forming, as they do, a new aristocracy of workers in a community whose
egalitarianism is only apparent.

All applicants are screened by the Illinois Department of Social Security, for information about their work record and basic skills. For those
who meet the preliminary criteria, the next step is the battery of state-
administered General Aptitude tests. After this, there is further screening
at the DSM Assessment Center. A physical examination and routine drug
test are also mandatory.

It goes against the grain for many people in the Mid-West to
acknowledge the industrial superiority of the Japanese. There is some
overt xenophobia, and an understandable reserve on the part of those who
were on the death marches of World War Two. Others insist that it is
now time for Japan to share the burden of defending the free world. There
is also much criticism of the Japanese for having unfairly protected their
industries. But perhaps the most common response would be familiar to
people in Britain; it clearly echoes the proprietorial tolerance with which
Britain once regarded the United States, seeing in it an extension of an
energy and vigour which originated in Britain. In the United States, the
reasoning goes like this: 'We are the true initiators and innovators, the
Japanese take over our inventions, improve upon them, perfect them.' In
this way, the Americans feel that they remain the true source of all that
is most vital in the world, even though they get less of the credit for it,
and little of the profit.

It turns out that Japanese management styles can be seen as simply a
matter of common sense. *Kaizen*, or 'continuous improvement', is at the
heart of the Mitsubishi philosophy, and who could quarrel with that? As
an employee of DSM, your advice and suggestions are sought for the
enhancement of safety and efficiency. All suggestions are considered; if
not implemented, you are given an explanation. It is easy to buy into such
a system, so different from traditional manufacturing plants, where
suggestions boxes grew dusty with disuse.

The training manual applies to all three thousand associates. There is
a common programme of work discipline. All wear the grey and maroon
uniform, which removes the last traces of any 'them and us' attitude. All
are part of the Diamond Star family. The United Autoworkers of America

(car workers union) was recognized by the company in December 1988; although it is hoped that in due course, the need for it will wither away.

The team concept pervades the plant. There are teams of 10–15 people, who all work together under a team-leader. Each team has 20–30 job responsibilities. People are trained in all of these, and the work is rotated on a two-hourly basis, so that each working day remains varied. It also means there is flexibility; if an associate is absent, someone can always cover. It is the antithesis of the monotony of the assembly-line, where people have always been given one simple, repetitive function. Naturally, the strong sense of belonging means that there are many collective social activities. On the Friday I was there, I was told 'Tomorrow some people are going to the ball-game in Peoria, there is a golf outing to Chicago, some of the women are shopping in Chicago, and there is a trip to the home of Abraham Lincoln in the state capital, Springfield.'

Among the employees are former bank-tellers, farmers, housewives, day care workers, students. Some have vocational qualifications, others university degrees. The level of educational attainment is relatively high; there is sophisticated equipment to operate, much information needs to be processed each day, there must be an ability to detect and analyse faults. No quality inspection is carried out until the vehicle is completed—the teams themselves are responsible for the quality, which is superb.

Donald Schoene is Executive Vice-President, Finance and Treasurer. Before joining Diamond Star, he spent more than twenty-five years with Chrysler, some as Controller for Chrysler, U.K. He says 'Our Eastern friends are very good at learning our Western trades. They know how to modify and enhance our technology. This places us in the role of teachers; and the knowledge we impart is then transferred back, improved, to the United States.' Don Schoene is thrilled by the way Japanese and Americans get along together:

> We had a baby shower for one member of the Finance Department, where there are four Japanese. Everybody joined in, we talked about baseball; some good friendships have developed. It is a great privilege to be able to learn about another culture through work.

While the robots take care of the work that is monotonous and danger-ous, the associates become responsible only for what is most creative:

There are three key words in Japanese: *muri* means 'unreasonable'; *mura* means 'uneven'; *muda* means 'unnecessary'. The approach is to remove all these from the workplace experience. This gains people's loyalty. In the past, the typical American plant would try to control waste by making the worker responsible for it; the workers became estranged from the company's ideals by having to do tasks that were not enhancing. The Japanese believe in consensual decision-making. This is also more efficient; our plant is two-thirds the size of the average American car-plant. We have two million square feet, producing two hundred and forty thousand cars a year, one thousand a day. The flow of work is so well-planned that it can be carried on in a smaller space. It is a process-driven product and plant.

When Diamond Star settled on Bloomington, they were anxious not to arrive in the Mid-West like a whirlwind. They wanted to stay on a par with the community, not offer sky-high wage-rates that would disrupt the local economy. Everything has been discreet and without ostentation. The wage-rates are comparable to those in the area, lower than in traditional assembly-plants. The associates are paid $9.95 an hour, and skilled maintenance people $11.74. DSM didn't want to strip other industries of their employees. Even so, there have been complaints in Peoria and Springfield that some heavy industrial works have lost people to DSM. The Japanese believe in *wa*, harmony among people at all levels, and have sought to insert themselves as unobtrusively as possible in Bloomington-Normal.

In spite of its compactness, the workplace is so big that it is difficult to see from one end of the building to the other. A subdued white light pervades the space, from where the great rolls of metal arrive in the press-shop, to the finished product. In the press-shop, the panels are delivered to a computer-controlled storage area; they are stored robotically, and distributed to the body-shop by automatic guided vehicles. Front and rear bumper fascias are moulded in the plastic shop. In the body shop, panels and undercarriage are welded together. There are more than two hundred and fifty robots, and ninety per cent of the operations here are automated. The conditions in the paint shop are said to be 'hospital clean'. More than seventy robots seal the welded seams of the car body. The doors are then removed, and the 'operating hardware' is installed; instrument panel, heater, air conditioner are also set in place automatically. There is a 'just in time' inventory management practice, which means that local suppliers can be alerted automatically when a new consignment of seats or tyres or some other component is due. This saves storage space.

The whole process moves forward at considerable speed; one vehicle is produced for every twenty-three work-hours. There is something disturbing about the robots; they are installed like some vast dismembering and disaggregation of a giant human body. They emerge from their place of rest in the form of skeletal arms, fingers, claws, eyes, an exposed musculature deftly lifting and placing with the greatest precision. Each movement goes forward at a precisely calculated pace, and is preceded by an electronic warning tune that sounds like 'Mary Had a Little Lamb', so that the employees can be clear of the arena of operation. When this is completed, the people move in to add their touch—so much lighter than the machines, so much more fragile than the robots, even than the power-tools, which are like multi-coloured intestinal tubes driving the instrument that bolts or rivets or seals. The vehicles emerge in such a way that those who work on the underside never have to bend down, but can work at eye level.

The guided vehicles taking the parts to the body shop emit a euphonic robotized warning as they go, following predetermined computerized tracks along the floor. Although it all seems smooth and effortless, enormous force is used; the robotic welding process, with its cascade of blue sparks, is noisy and dazzling; the hammering and thud of the metal each time the whole ensemble moves forward demand ear-plugs, hard hats and goggles. There is little room for the employees to communicate beyond co-ordinating their specific function. Some of the operations are spectacularly graceful—the double- or triple-jointed flexibility of metal arms that lift the windshield with suction-pads and dexterously place it in the aperture of the car-frame is part of an impressive choreography of robotics.

Yet the subordination of the people to the process remains; the dwarfing, indeed the inferiorizing of human beings, who must wait until the warning music comes, and then, with precision, accomplish their task, and then withdraw, so that the whole lot can proceed to the next work-station. Even the instrument panel is robotically installed, concluded by the oversight of a bulging cyclopean electronic eye. Each vehicle is inspected at the end, subjected to a water test. As soon as it goes into the storage yard, it becomes the property of the distributor.

There are two eight-hour shifts at present, with a forty-two minute meal-break (this because time is measured in tenths of one hour). The shifts begin at 7.0 a.m. and 3.0 p.m., and are preceded by ninety seconds of stretching exercises. Thirty-five per cent of the associates are women. Most are young. There has been only one serious accident so far— one associate thought a robot was in a training mode—i.e. was still being taught the operation it had to perform, when it was already in the production mode.

That production can take place with such scant human intervention is both exalting and appalling; exalting because it makes the possibilities seem endless; appalling, because so little of the labour saved is of any benefit to all the underoccupied and unemployed all over the world.

The finished product, the Eclipse and the Laser, stand on plinths in the reception area, a place of bare, functional metal and marble, with only photographs of the Illinois countryside on the walls as a sort of reminder of the location of the plant.

The embodiment of such power and strength in these robots represents the successful neutralization of the working class; it celebrates the triumph of the international capital which has, contrary to some predictions, proved itself to be the gravedigger of labour. This is perhaps the meaning of that dispersal of disembodied energies and powers in these tame machines. The flesh and blood has been liberated into the benign functions required by the service economy of Bloomington-Normal. No wonder the associates of DSM are required to have intelligence, communicative ability and psycho-social skills; as well as doing their job, their role is also that of custodians of the funerary monument of a defunct working class.

Poor in a Rich Town

Many people in McLean County are emphatic: there is no poverty here. Some will qualify this judgment, and say that if there are poor, this is because they won't work, or because they drink too much. The majority regard the social and economic system which has served them so well as just about perfect; the only problem is those individuals, too wilful or too stupid to avail themselves of the benefits it showers upon the people.

Even the poorest rarely define themselves as such; they are 'low-income people', in spite of the fact that twenty per cent of American families have an income lower than $5,107 a year. The least advantaged, the relatively deprived—whatever euphemism is employed—feel ashamed of their lack of resources; which is why so many of them are anxious to dissociate themselves from the odious taint of poverty. In this way, a collusion exists between the possessing classes and the have-nots, as united in their denial of poverty as in their search for more wealth. It is difficult to imagine more elegant arrangements for the conduct of society, whereby the poor are so ready to acquiesce in their own invisibility.

Perhaps this is what Mary Campbell—who works with the homeless—meant, when she spoke of the 'loneliness of poverty'. For it goes without saying that if the poor conceal their privations from the rich, they will be at pains to do likewise with their peers. They are left to brood privately upon their lack of worth—both market and moral—assailed as they are, from all sides, by an iconography of luxury and wealth. When they do try to make sense of society, they are more likely to become resentful of the imagined advantages of other low-income groups than to blame the absence of social justice. Whites turn against Blacks ('They get whatever they ask for from Public Aid'), young against old ('They ride their trailers round the country like they don't have a care in the world'), the childless against families ('I couldn't get Public Aid because I didn't have the foresight to get me an illegitimate kid'). What is worse, the poor seem more vulnerable to the fragility, and consequent break-up of families; a disproportionate number of people blamed parents, siblings, children, for their misfortunes.

As American society grows richer, the gap between rich and poor widens, and not only in monetary terms; the poor also become more deskilled. It is estimated that functional illiteracy has reached thirty per cent (officially around thirteen per cent); while 1988 saw thirty-eight million recorded crimes, perhaps the most telling index of despair.

As the labour process becomes more minutely sub-divided, people know more and more about reduced areas of expertise. This intense specialization seriously depowers them in relation to an ever-wider range of experience in which they have no competence. This scarcely matters to those with high and rising incomes, those whose restricted but detailed knowledge guarantees them ample reward, and who can 'buy in' anything they lack, can make good from a constantly expanding range of goods and services any deficiency in their ability to provide what they need. Unfortunately, the poor are condemned to inhabit the same culture; they are subject to the same process of dispossession in terms of skills, but they have neither the money nor the acquired ability to get the job that will help them redress the glaring insufficiencies of their lives.

In spite of the rhetoric of the Reagan years, programmes such as Headstart, for pre-school children, supplemental food programmes for women, infants and children, were not dismantled; to have done so might have laid bare some of the more baleful consequences of the dynamics of wealth-creation. Many young parents in the United States are little more than children themselves; children bringing up children. Is it any wonder that nutritionists must be employed by social programmes in an attempt to counter the more effective information disseminated by free enterprise—the purveyors of instant satisfactions and fast foods that leave so many children both overweight and undernourished? The growth and expansion of the food industry can be measured in the obesity of people, who must then be slimmed down by another group of entrepreneurs, whose business is with medicines and the restoration of health. Sometimes, it seems, people are being processed, like the food they eat.

Basic deficiencies in education come from the fact that the poor have been instructed, not principally by the schools, but by the publicists of enterprises for whom the needs of the economy take precedence over the care of human beings. Ruth Wantling, who works for Community Action in Bloomington, describes what is happening:

There are many families for whom food preparation is a lost art. Cooking has become a gourmet skill, a hobby for those who choose it. Eating out is the norm for many families. Craft skills are also a kind of ornament, not part of the fabric of life—sewing, dressmaking, repairing goods, making and growing things—are part of the leisure of the well-to-do, not integrated into the strategies of daily survival of the poor.

If this were not so, how would it be possible that brick and concrete structures, often of bleak and forbidding aspect, come to bear the sign 'Human Resource Centers'?

This by-product of the evolution of the market system has been relatively little observed by commentators. When universal scarcity was a threat to the survival of large numbers of people, increases in production seemed the sole concern of all economic endeavour. That the further elaboration of the division of labour seemed the key to this was understandable, as in Adam Smith's panegyric:

> The division of labour . . . so far as it can be introduced, occasions, in every art, a proportionate increase of the productive powers of labour. The separation of different trades and employments from one another seems to have taken place in consequence of this advantage. This separation, too, is generally carried furthest in those countries which enjoy the highest degree of industry and improvement; what is the work of one man in a rude state of society being generally that of several in an improved one. In every improved society, the farmer is generally nothing but a farmer; the manufacturer nothing but a manufacturer. The labour, too, which is necessary to produce any one complete manufacture is almost always divided among a great number of hands.*

While the basic problem remained one of global material scarcity, the further development of the division of labour seemed the most desirable goal of society. Partly in consequence of its success, and partly because the economic system which gave rise to its expansion was articulated, not

---

* Adam Smith, *The Wealth of Nations*, (Penguin Books, London, 1983)

to answering need, but to the expansion of profit, we now see new conditions created as a consequence. The inability of people to cope with life outside the cash economy is one factor which could not possibly have been foreseen by the early enthusiasts of the market. The dependency it generates is a novel, but inescapable contemporary disabling force.

Perhaps this is why so many poor people keep their television permanently tuned to the selling channel, which is on air day and night. Even the 'shut-ins' (the housebound, the very old, the afraid, the agoraphobic) can still participate, even if vicariously, in this most basic activity of social life. Conversations with the poor were accompanied by some surreal television interventions, which only served to emphasize their condition of dependent exclusion.

Grace lives in a public housing scheme, a modest development of 'row-houses' (terraces) on the edge of town. A warm, generous woman, born with only one arm, she has known struggle all her life:

> My Mom and Dad gave me to my grandparents when I was just an itty-bitty thing. I always wanted to be an attorney, but my mother sent me to a convent. I ran the streets and got pregnant. I had three kids, but my mother had them taken away from me. I left them with my grandmother one night, but when I got home, they'd gone. She called me an unfit mother. She had a lot to talk about. I tried hard to love her, but I could do nothing right. I have so much resentment and hatred. She called me a one-armed sonofabitch, said she wouldn't even walk down the street with me.

The television at this point is offering a crystal-glass piano with love-birds; five alabaster eggs on stands as 'collectables'; a family heirloom clock, which your grandchildren will be proud to inherit. There are wonderful new 'eye products', and 'exciting lip-therapy'. There is a telephone in the form of a model Ferrari. ('You can never have too many telephones in your home.')

'When I'm dead and in my grave', says Grace, 'nobody will know I existed. My boy is twenty-three. He's been in trouble for drugs and alcohol. He was just arrested, driving under the influence. He could get 1–3 years. The mother of his child has taken their little Sharika and gone to Wisconsin. That little girl was my baby; everything I have has been taken away.' Grace's eyes fill with tears; on the wall is a picture of the two-year-old, tucked inside the frame of a larger photo of Grace. 'She was running round on my boy, taking Sharika with her to get drunk. I get upset when the child isn't here, and I get upset when her mother is.'

'We are in the information age', the television persists, offering items to store knowledge, to retain memories; it fails to add that that knowledge and those memories must first be separated from the brain that is perfectly capable of containing them. 'This is state of the art. An automatic dialler . . . If you don't have a CD player, you'll be passed by.'

Grace follows her own train of thought:

> The law in this town is bullcrap. If you have a scanner, you can listen to the cops on the radio. They make fun of people. Anyone with a mental disorder is referred to as 'the crazy one'. They say 'We'll go and see the jungle bunnies', that kind of stuff. Anyone who lives in public housing is trash, to them this is Trash City.

Many poor people, to avoid the stigma of public housing, live in trailer parks. Oak Park is on the far periphery of Bloomington; about sixty trailers, mostly white or cream, parked around a rough road in the shape of a horse-shoe. Joe Henneberger is a thin young man of twenty-five. The third of nine children, he was brought up in a boys' home in Ohio, later fostered by a family in Bloomington. He left school after eleventh grade, worked washing dishes, cooking, and then as security guard. He has been married to Cheryl since he was eighteen; there is a little girl of five, and a three-month-old baby, who is lying on the thick-pile carpet that covers the trailer floor. Joe has taught himself television repair and maintenance; the trailer is stacked with parts, repaired and half-repaired televison sets. Most have come from trash cans or were picked up for a few dollars. Joe can't under-stand why he can't get work repairing televisions. Because he has no qual-ifications, no one will employ him, even though he is perfectly competent. Cheryl works three days a week, cleaning for $4.25 an hour at Pine Crest apartments.

'There is always a mis-match between the rates of pay of the labour market and what is considered the acceptable standard of living in the community', says Ruth Wantling. If Joe Henneberger were a more attent-ive monitor of the market, he might know that the mending of disposable objects is barely profitable. He might listen instead to the expressed needs of the well-to-do, like the wealthy realtor who said 'Busy families like mine, where we both work, sub-contract our lives.' The millions of jobs created during the Reagan era were designed to service such people; much of the work is casual, part-time, low-paid, without medical insurance, over-whelmingly for women and young people; poverty in the United States has, accordingly, been increasingly concentrated in these groups. Their work is not only in restaurants, hotels and kitchens, in janitorial and sec-urity jobs, but also in providing services which people previously either performed quite competently for themselves, or had not seen as economic activity at all. It is now possible to make a living planning other people's dinner parties, advising them how to dress, how to shop; there are consul-tants in pet nutrition, facilitators and accessorizers, conjurors of services out of thin air. The realtor who sub-contracts his life reminded me of Oscar Wilde's aphorism: 'Living? Our servants can do that for us'. No doubt, those whose job it is to offer a choice of lemon, lime or pine-scented spray inside your vehicle at the car-wash, who will stand in line for you at the supermarket, who will address you in sexy little-girl voices ('Hello, I'm Kelly and I'll be your hostess this evening') at the restaurant, bestow an agreeable sense of enlargement upon the lives of those they service. But occasionally, the overstretched division of labour snaps, as it did for the distraught mother who had to take her sick child to the baby-sitter 'because she knows her so much better than I do', or for the parents who find themselves distributing printed notes on their children's pillows say-ing 'I Love You', in the absence of more direct communication.

When Joe Henneberger says all he wants is a job with a fair wage, with medical cover for his children, he is asserting human need over economic necessity; a struggle that never dies, however discouraging the outcome sometimes seems.

> I don't care about myself. If I break my arm I don't go to hospital. But I want my kids looked after. I don't think of myself as poor. People call me trash-picker, but that is because the stuff they throw out isn't trash—it's new. The picture flickers on the television screen, so they junk it and buy another. There's nothing in this trailer that's new. I got the microwave for $14, the white AMC Pacer outside for $20.

It isn't fair. Blacks on Public Aid, they drive up in Cadillacs, one white kid, one Black and one Mexican, and they get away with it. It's a bunch of crap. If I get a job, we'll have to pay $17 a day for a child-minder. You can't trust anyone, there's a lot of child-molesters around. I did two and a half years in jail for burglary, but it did me a lot of good. Low-income people get picked on. A neighbour in the trailer park where we were called the Department of Children and Family Services. They accused us of not feeding our daughter. She was five, and weighed only thirty pounds. But I only weigh one hundred pounds myself. I'm not having my kids taken away. If they try anything, they better bring an army with them. I was taken from my parents for alcohol and neglect. I've been a drinker myself, and I've proved that you can kick it, because I have. I don't like this town, all these students, they don't know their arsehole from a hole in the ground. I want to go to school, study digital electronics; if I can't, we'll leave this State, take off for Florida.

Henry Schultz Jnr. has even more archaic ideas about working life. He was raised on a farm, where his father was a tenant-farmer. The farm was long ago demolished and incorporated into a larger unit. Henry remembers working from the age of about six, helping his father birth the calves, herbal remedies of catnip for colic, a buckeye for rheumatism. He forecasts the weather from signs in nature—rabbits running mean rain, a bad winter if squirrels' tails are bushier than usual. He carries a radio with him, and listens to every weather-cast. Henry lives with his brother, brother's wife and their three children. The small wooden house is very cluttered: the rooms taken up by bunk-beds, double beds, big sofa, chairs, television table. Much of the clutter is junk; a giant plastic tomato is an ice-holder, there are jugs, model houses, cards, gauzy flowers covered with dust, plastic trucks and pails, rubber bones for the dogs, metal miniature cars, glass fish, clocks, plaster figures, photographs, candle-holders, light-fittings, rose-bowls; yesterday's novelties.

It is perhaps no accident that the story told by many poor people is about the ruin of their relationships; it sometimes seems that the human occupants are being evicted from their lives to make way for so much junk and garbage. If their tale is about who conned them and cheated and fooled them, lied to them, betrayed them and abandoned them, their concerns find an echo in the television programmes—which are watched for an average of about seven hours a day in American homes—that sustain a litany of disgraced humanity; couples confessing their infidelity to each other, therapists advising frightened and lonely people how to make a relationship, how to keep a man, get a girlfriend, make their children love them; how to make themselves desirable, stay sexy, cheat the ageing process, become more interesting, hold themselves together. People confide their most shaming secrets to the television cameras; their unspoken desires, their disgraceful lusts and inadmissable longings all become public property. Is it any wonder that they say they feel empty inside, hollow, there is nothing left? There is, it seems, no holding back the torrent of confessions, the voiding of the inner substance; we are invited to be present at an incontinent and orgiastic emotional evisceration. The inner spaces are being cleared, with the result that even the most tawdry purchase will look like a consolation and a restorative. The ground of the inner landscape is being broken for new poverties, receptive to the vast freight of commodities, services, bought-in compensations still slumbering within the inexhaustible reservoir of capitalist invention and becoming. The sense of poverty, in even the richest places that live under the dominion of the markets remains elusive, hard to apprehend, yet persistent, wounding, long after it has been declared cured, non-existent.

It isn't a poverty of possession so much as a poverty of power. Those who have no choice but to enter into the value-added servitude of other people's purchasing-power, speak, above all, of their feeling of *impotence*: Corinne, cleaner at a motel at $3.30 an hour, never knowing how many hours she will work each day—it all depends on the level of room occupancy. 'You start at seven, you might work three, five, seven hours. But you never know how much your pay-check is going to be. You can't budget, you can't plan.' Judy works on the reception desk of a motel that the State Farm Insurance Company uses as training centre for its employees. She is paid $3.75 an hour; over a third of her gross income goes for a small apartment, where the thermostat on the heating is locked at sixty degrees Fahrenheit even in winter. A man who lost his job when Funk's Seeds were taken over by Ciba-Geigy, owns a transit van worth more than $5,000 and cannot therefore get Public Aid unless he sells it; he is helped by the labour of his children—the fifteen-year-old helps a roofer at weekends, while the thirteen-year-old works in a restaurant every day after school. At 7 a.m. in the Union Hall of the Labourers International Union of America, construction workers seeking a day's labour wait for news of hirings. Tom McLaughlin says 'It costs me two thousand dollars just to get up every morning.' He is married but without children; there is, he says, too much misery in the world to bring children into it—violence, child-abuse, AIDS, drugs. He saw what happened to his own mother, when their father died—she was left with six kids to bring up on her own. Fred Shield is a serious young man in his twenties. He worked for an asbestos company owned by a relative, but had to go into dangerous buildings with no masks or respirator; and he was always away from home and never saw his wife and four-year-old daughter. Later, he worked for a packaging company. One day, undoing a wire-bound package, the wire band sprang up and cut his eye; he had an eye-lens transplant, but received no compensation.

Mike Matijka of the Labourers International says we must expect to see intensified poverty. Only twenty per cent of American workers are now unionized. It is scarcely that workers no longer need protection, with capital as powerful as it is—it is simply that new patterns of labour are harder to organize, the service sector too diffuse and mobile. Work is becoming more dangerous, more casualized, less well-paid.

In the United States, poverty means the dispersal of the poor, the construction of poverty as a problem for individuals, which prevents collective recognition and action. It is a poverty in which the poor dare not even name themselves, and which is, therefore, secure against any imaginable remedy.

13 / MARKET ANALYSIS

EVEN ON ITS OWN TERMS, the market economy fails to live up to many of its promises. There is, in Western society, a deep contradiction between the sovereignty of the individual and the mass markets through which those individuals must express themselves; for mass markets, despite their vaunted sensitivity and sophistication, tend to greater standardization and uniformity. Their diversity is largely illusion, little more than variations in packaging rather than content, and the success of any new item depends for its success on such extravagant promotional investment that it ensures that those who can invest large sums in marketing have a disproportionate advantage over everyone else.

Freedom of choice has become a rallying cry in the West; this is what is supposed to distinguish us from the drab sameness and chronic inefficiency of those countries which call themselves socialist. We may wonder how it comes about that all those ostensibly free choices tend in aggregate to settle on identical products, services and purchases, television programmes, items of food, newspapers, pop stars, films promoted by a handful of transnational entities? What is the secret that turns so many free individuals into frightened emulation and conformism? How do choices become structured in such a way that what the people want happens to coincide so painlessly with what the market system can provide? It sometimes seems, less that the goods have been delivered to the people than that the people have been delivered to the goods, their sensibility refashioned in such a way that all its felt longings and absences correspond precisely to what is available for money. The violence that this profound manipulation may do to human beings does not appear in the marketplace, but is perhaps to be counted in the toll of wounded and damaged people who express their pain and anger only through the statistics of social breakdown, crime and psychiatric and emotional illness.

Mass markets clearly have an important cohesive function; not only do they filter even greater concentrations of wealth towards the already rich, the representatives of powerful parastatal companies and conglomerates, but they also provide meaning for the people who seek satisfaction through them. Perhaps participation in mass markets has become an alternative to other forms of solidaristic endeavour which have been undermined in our time. There are, after all, fewer spaces in which collective action is possible. The trades unions have been significantly weakened; and in any case, they had already shown themselves to be little more than competitive organizations for groups of workers to fight over the spoils of capitalism. Any claims they might have made to higher purposes of social transformation have lapsed, and are now passed over in rigorous silence.

Yet the needs of people to belong to something greater than those fragile and often unstable units of belonging to which they have access in our fragmented society have not disappeared merely because the labour movement has seen its sometime long-term goals attenuated or by-passed. Mass markets serve as a focus for illusions of shared and participatory activity. In this process, the peer group becomes a kind of substitute for community, and the desire to belong in an atrophied culture finds its principal outlet in shared styles, fashions, heroes, television programmes, brand loyalties, shopping habits and addictions. Controlled and manufactured experience stands us in the stead of more organic involvement in community, neighbourhood or social struggle. The norms are provided by our immediate reference-group, which comes to mean those with similar incomes who spend their money on the same purchased experiences, and who impose their will, as severe, compelling and constraining as the most narrow-minded village or street community, the most orthodox suburban propriety. The markets are another, more subtle form of privatization; the privatization of collective activity, and its reconstitution in the realm of fantasy. For instance, it is the people in the television soap operas who provide the easy and accessible familiarity of neighbourhood; while in the actual places where people live, they tell you of the fear on the streets, of doors barricaded against intruders, of violence and distrust, of the strangers who live next door. You can gossip about and dissect the behaviour of those in *Eastenders*, *Neighbours* or *Dallas* without wounding anyone, without danger of reprisals. There is no commitment and no consequences; you can express moral disapproval without expecting a brick through the window in response. You can experience a sterile and lonely tenderness over the fate and suffering of figures known to everyone, but for whom no one has any responsibility. Where real flesh and blood is so intractable, difficult, or simply tediously repetitive, we can shed a cathartic tear, indulge a fond smile, secure in an enclosed emotional autism which we share with millions. Similarly, as fans of a singer or a group or a celebrity, we enjoy both a sense of safety and a feeling of participation in some public arena. Further, we recognize an elective kindred in those who have recourse to the same style, who cultivate the same image, buy at the same store, fill their houses with the same objects—or in only the slightest variants of them, which offer such agreeable scope for mild disagreements and interesting discussion. The nationally published popular press is the noticeboard of this neighbourhood of nowhere, these friendships of fantasy, which are the principal socially approved forms of collective activity in the world.

The cults that grow around mass markets are deeply conservative and profoundly dependent. They exist solely within and because of present patterns of production and distribution. The development of a single European market, let alone of a global market, suggests anything but concern for individuals. Their personal choices are transformed, by the hidden hand, not into universal well-being, but into an inturned and passive expression of collective activity, or rather, impotence; shared experience, but one that remains subordinate, and this has little to do with any traditional solidaristic purposes. There is no questioning, no challenge to existing structures of wealth and power. It can accommodate no visions of change, no alternatives, other than slight mutations of what already exists. Yesterday's fashion, styles and tastes become instant nostalgia, a substitute for history; tomorrow's novelties and distractions the source of our best hopes for the future, a surrogate for hopeful action for change. Mass markets are capitalism's degraded version of solidarities it has broken, of human belonging it has brought to ruin.

And yet, the markets are the most reliable expression of what the people want, or so we are told by those who see in them the hand of Providence, a reflection of the laws of nature, which are also the laws of God; the most perfect arrangements in a fallible world for the regulation of human affairs. Indeed *what the people want* is a clarion call, the unappealable court of last resort in a democracy. It is a slogan ruthlessly employed, both to defend all existing evils and to suppress dissent. *What the people want* has been sacralized; even though, throughout most of recorded history, what the people want is precisely what their rulers have spared no effort to withhold from them. This change is offered as evidence of the enlightenment of this age; but it does prompt the question of how this happy congruence should have been achieved between the wants of the people and what had always been regarded as economic necessity.

For one thing, it is clear that the markets furnish only a fraction of what the people want. People also want more compassion, less social cruelty, a more just distribution of wealth. But they cannot have them. Instead, they must listen to the hymning of the hidden hand, even as its grip tightens around the throat of so many of their fellow-citizens. What they can have is what is available, and to this they must learn to shape their wants; and this means, above all, to whatever supremely dispensable vanity makes its appearance on the market. That this is so readily accepted—as a consolation for who knows what comforts and experiences and needs that have been suppressed because of their impossibility of transformation into marketed form—is then cited as proof that the markets faithfully reflect the profoundest yearnings of the people.

People also do not want so much violence, crime, fear, loneliness and addiction. They don't want child abuse, attacks on women, assaults on the elderly. They would prefer not to see such extensive emotional and psychological breakdown, such stress, despair and ruin of families. The fact that these unsolicited presences seem to be the inseparable companions of what the people most deeply desire is an awkward contradiction; what they *don't* want has never been part of the deal. What people can have are the joys and pleasures of spending; however real these may prove, some cruel and unwanted phenomena attend them, which will not be shaken off. In compensation, people are offered more credit and more economic growth.

It seems that the price paid for the freedoms the markets bestow is somewhat heavier than the mere monetary cost of each article or service so swiftly used up and forgotten. The essence of market transactions is their instantaneity. They occur in a perspectiveless present, and all long-term consequences are excluded, many of which are equally unwanted— the poisonings and pollutions of the elements that sustain life, the depletions of the world which our children will inherit, the unfreedoms which today's free choices bring to the poor of the earth.

There are other, equally important objections to the myth that free markets are the emancipators of humanity. For one thing, freedom of choice is propounded as though it were an absolute, existing in a world of theoretic and ahistorical purity, at a moment without antecedent, uninfluenced by anything that had gone before. And yet, the choices of yesterday have already had their effects; their consequences become a major determinant upon the present, and upon the next generation who must grow up in the environment shaped by them. The markets have become a dominant— even overwhelming—aspect of the raising of children in the West. The choices which children make occur in a context heavily structured by the results and the aftermath of the choices of others. Above all, what they learn is that what is available in the world is to be had only for money. How could it occur to a consciousness so penetrated by this powerful lesson that there might be things in the world that money cannot buy? When adults feel that money is the measurable token of good parenting, is it any wonder that the young grow up receptive to that construction of the world offered by those who would offer consumer choices as the essence of all human liberties?

Why then has the market place become the object of such reverence? It is, without doubt, the most dynamic and salient feature of Western society. When something so powerful and ubiquitous pervades the lives of the people, it is easy to mistake its strength, not only for truth, but for morality also. Since there exists no other source of values that can compete with the vigour of the markets, these absorb something of the awe and wonder with which people once contemplated the forces of nature.

Markets, which are—or should be— neutral, impersonal, instrumental, merely a useful mechanism for bringing together buyers and sellers, have taken on a portentous and inconceivable role in rich Western society: they have become the arbiters of good and evil. What makes money is good, regardless of the consequences—carcinogens, weaponry, toxins in the food chain that contaminate people and earth alike; while what fails in the market-place, that arena where every day is a day of judgement, quickly disappears from the crowded window-displays, even if it is something indispensable to human survival. But perhaps the greatest triumph of the markets has been to have muted certain forms of struggle, collective action and resistance to the necessities of capitalism; to have broken these things and reconstructed them in its own image, within the very system against which they were once mobilized.

The labour market degraded and deformed human lives—and continues to do so all over the world—through the operation of what were regarded as its immutable laws. Now we in the West have been bidden to believe that markets have been purified, metamorphosed into the surest guarantors of human freedom and happiness. Yet their workings, even in the rich consumer societies are no less radically mis-shaping and distorting than they are in the cities of the Third World. The very notion that the primary purpose of human beings in the world is that of consumers—the eager devourers of as many resources as they can use up in a lifetime—is no more emancipating than their existence as the mere hands of this or that manufactory. Markets have not changed—the locus where they work their greatest harm may shift from society to society, from one place to another—but what broke and destroyed human lives in the West, and still does so in the countries of the South, cannot liberate them in a few favoured corners of the world.

It may well be that the trades union and labour movements have become tired and exhausted, an inadequate form of resistance to the profuse and subtle forms of dispossession and loss to which free markets subject a humanity unprotected from their unchecked expression all over the earth. We may wonder where we shall find the energies, the will and the strength that once animated the defenders of a Western working-class now grown somnolent, in order to combat the desolation they leave in their wake, the multiple scars on the face of the planet, and in the lives of the people, rich and poor alike. The work of resistance may have faltered for a time; the emergence of the Green movement is an indication that it has not died, but is simply re-forming in a shape more appropriate to the monstrous scale on which markets are free and human beings their captives.

14/ SOCIAL DEMOCRACY
AND ITS ENVIRONMENT

THE CURIOUS SEPARATION of social issues from the economic system which creates them could never have occurred but for the contribution of reformers and improvers of the past. Among these, the role of social democratic parties has been the most significant of all. This is not, of course, to speak of betrayals of the working class or of collusion with capitalism, as some on the left have done. There is no doubt that all the reforms which those in, for instance, the Labour Party in Britain worked and struggled for, were pursued in good faith. It is simply that the ways in which these were deformed by the context in which they had to exist were not foreseen. However, the point has now been reached when the consequence of the improvements can no longer be ignored. Nowhere can the process of absorption and deformation be more clearly seen than in that most resonant area of social democratic change which sought to alter the 'environment' of the classic industrial working class.

Against those, who, in the early industrial era, argued that the poverty of the working class was nothing more than a reflection of their own moral worth (or lack of it), socialists claimed that it was the environmental disabilities of health, housing and education which made the working class incapable of competing on the same terms as those whose lives were burdened by no such disadvantages, and who found their way to wealth and power, not without effort certainly, but without the impediment of these social obstacles. Indeed, the argument between left and right—particularly before the great reforms of the post-war period—came to resolve itself into an act of faith as to the relative importance of environment and inheritance as determinant upon the poverty of the mass of the people.

To read Tawney on equality* in the 1980s is to catch a glimpse of the conviction of those most passionate socialists who argued that a complete transformation in the circumstances of the lives of the poorest would abolish those inequalities that were a focus of such resentment on the one hand, and for such fearful contempt on the other. He wrote in 1931:

> If every individual were reared in conditions as favourable to health as science can make them, received an equally thorough and stimulating education up to the age of sixteen, and knew on reaching manhood (sic) that, given a reasonable measure of hard work and good fortune, could face the risks of life without being crushed by them, the most shocking of existing inequalities would be on the way to disappear.

With what triumph the right has been able to point to the disappearance of the old industrial squalors, and to the subsequent survival—indeed, in recent years, the aggravation—of inequalities, and to cite this as evidence, if not as proof positive, that it is not, after all, the environment that lies at the root of the suffering of the poor! What we have seen, in the post-war era, has been nothing less than what appears to be a conclusive demonstration of the falsehood of those tenets of faith of social democracy, that if only the living-conditions and life-chances of the poor could be improved, they would then be well able to compete with those not so disfavoured, and that, as a result, a far greater measure of equality would be attained.

A complete transformation of the environment did indeed occur. But that change was in fact a counterfeit, a mere semblance of that anticipated by socialists. It was a perversion, a shadow of the change for which they had worked, although they did not recognize it as such at the time; and this is why it has been derided, scorned by the right, as though it really had represented the ambitions of a Tawney, the dreams of a William Morris, the visions of the early Labour movement. The changed decor has been held up to demonstrate definitively the impossibility of trying to redeem the irredeemable, the folly of efforts to raise up those whose true element remains the mire. This bogus transformation, presided over in

* R.H.Tawney, *Equality*, (Penguin)

large measure by those proud to call themselves socialists, has cut the ground from under the feet of those who have come after in ways which they have been unable to come to terms with. For socialists are left proclaiming the same message which they were preaching before the great changes occurred, and which sounds so strangely archaic now. For the capitalist environment, although transformed beyond the imaginings of the early socialists, is no more a guarantor of greater equality than would have been the exchange of a stone prison for a metal cage, however gilded.

It was a perhaps understandable error of socialists to have believed that certain existential ameliorations—improved health, lengthened life expectancy, protection from hunger and cold—would, of themselves, offer a safe passage to the working poor through the capitalist jungle, as they competed on equal terms with their sometime betters. This now appears to have been a fallacy. The old industrial squalor has been largely demolished; yet the benign social consequences which ought to have followed have somehow failed to appear in any enduring way. Indeed, the abatement of the existential disadvantages has only revealed other, less tractable forms of injury and damage to people which are just as prejudicial to their ability to compete as anything that went before.

Tawney's postscript to the 1952 edition of *Equality* accepted that all was not perfect, but he serenely anticipated that this was simply a question of time, that the mechanisms already in place would in the long run produce the effects that had been foreseen; this, doubtless, was what Labour Party leaders came to call 'the nuts and bolts', the 'fine tuning' of the welfare state. What we, in 1990, must state quite clearly is that the failure of the expected liberation to show itself is evidence, not of the inferior moral qualities of the poor, as is implied (and sometimes made quite explicit) by the right, in its public and hypocritical sorrowing over the blemishes of an unregenerate and unalterable human nature, but rather that the corrupting and disabling power of the capitalist environment—even though changed beyond recognition from its 'classical' nineteenth century shape—has easily survived the mere re-arrangement of the scenery that has been the object of so much comment since the Second World War.

That the modified setting of their lives, the altered function and transformed material circumstances might also manage to impoverish the spirit, to undermine the self-reliance, to deter people's faith in their own powers, to recreate (even though in different guise) so many of the barbarities of Victorian social life, was not among the expectations of most early socialists. The elimination of certain features of those damaging nineteenth century landscapes have indeed led to improved health and better chances of survival; but other, depowering and destructive characteristics have been inserted into even that transformed material environment. Perhaps this could not have been foreseen by the visionaries and pioneers of the labour movement. Their concerns were perhaps too immediate; although it must be admitted that William Morris, for one, was well aware that there was more to socialism than work, welfare and municipal parks. Shortly before he died, William Morris gave a lecture, called 'What We Have to Look For'. He said:

> I should, above all things, like to have an answer to this question; setting aside all convention, all rhetoric and flummery, what is it that you want from the present labour movement? Higher wages, more regular employment? Shorter working hours—better education for your children—old age pensions, libraries, parks and the rest? Are these, and things like them, what you want? They are, of course, *but what else do you want?* If you cannot answer the question straightforwardly, I must say you are wandering on a road, the outcome of which you cannot tell.

But we, who live on the other side of that prophecy, and have lived through the demolition of those industrial sites of exploitation and despair, can see where that road has led. Many people, turning in bewilderment to the old texts, have sought comfort in the sulphurous denunciations of Engels, or the subtle ironies of Tawney, as though such profound mutations as we have witnessed had not really occurred, as though we could expect to meet, on the other side of the great transformations, the same people, with the same sensibility, as those who laboured throughout the first industrial era. All we have to do, say the fundamentalists of the left, is 'to go back to our roots', to uncover the old texts, just as the fundamentalists of the right have done so successfully in the 1980s, and there we shall find the inspiration and spur to action.

It should be apparent by now that this is not enough. It is the task of true radicals to be alive to, to name and describe, to isolate and denounce the cause of the evils of this age, evils that have, as it were, been refracted through the very reforms that we have known and welcomed. We should not be afraid to speak of the decay of a culture which is dominated by an ideology that teaches that life is something out of which it is the individual's highest duty to get as much money, sex and fun as he or she may; the dehumanizing of people in what is mistakenly called 'popular culture' (for it belongs to capitalism) in its 'entertainment' industry, with its cult of violence and pornography and degradation of human relationships; the cynicism of the morality of money (good is having plenty and evil is having none); the debauch of the imagination of the young; the stifling of their powers and creativity through the universal imagery of shadowy stars and heroes. It is for us to show how such phenomena are products of that 'better world' which was fought for so valiantly, and of which our children are the pitiable inheritors; how that better world has proved to be a travesty of what was to have been, and how its principal function has been to preserve all the features of an older, worse world.

Many on the left have been able to do little more than fulminate against 'poverty' or 'unemployment' in the presence of so many other, less familiar evils—less familiar because they have accompanied capitalism's version of riches. The rhetoric of the left has proved inadequate to rouse the people against the cruelties of contemporary capitalist society. The task is more subtle and more difficult. Those who have continued to employ an archaic language to denounce known wrongs have done so simply because these are known, and therefore, in a way, comforting. Their most grave fault has been to believe that all has been revealed, and that they have nothing more to learn. Those for whom revelation is the guide to action are rarely equipped to deal adequately with actually existing phenomena, however glaring and scandalous these may be. Tawney would perhaps have been equal to the challenge. 'The most singular phenomenon', he wrote, 'can be made to pass unchallenged, provided that the minds of observers have been tuned to regard them as inevitable and edifying.' And while such manifestations as drug abuse, violence against children, the fragility of our commitment to one another, the multiple addictions—of which by far the greatest is to money—are scarcely edifying, they are certainly regarded as inevitable. Indeed, it is the suspicion that these are all part of the hidden price that must be paid for the 'better life' of which we are always being told we are the happy beneficiaries, that has imposed a taboo, an absolute proscription upon looking at their source and origin, and which inhibits us from saying what needs to be done with the radical honesty and vigour which Tawney devoted to his denunciations of inequality.

Much of what Tawney wrote in the 1930s sounds ironic, mocking, disturbing, now. The changes in that blighted industrial environment that Labour fought for did indeed create a new landscape; what a paradox it is that this 'environment' should have been the terrain on which the reformist zeal of social democracy was destined to struggle and has been seen to falter; the more so since the triumph of capitalism has been at the expense of the wider, natural environment on which it is both parasitic and dependent.

If environment has become again the site of struggle, this is because the altered decor that capitalism has created has been artificially imposed upon the natural world, on which all economic systems ultimately depend. The technosphere has obscured the biosphere. One consequence of this is that the real environment has been obscured for a majority of the people by the garish and showy artefact that has been substituted for it. Social democracy, having colluded with the earlier reforms, is ill-placed to develop a convincing critique of this more urgent crisis confronting the world now.

It has been the inglorious fate of the Labour Party to have led those it thought of as its own people into the stifling embrace of a system which, rather than jeopardize one atom of the wealth and power of the rich, would risk the extinction of the whole planet. That those people who, in the early years of struggle, formulated only the desire for sufficiency for all, should have been harnessed to the need for growth and expansion of an industrialism that ravages the natural base on which it rests, is a sad and bitter experience. No longer harnessed to the engines of economic growth like beasts through their labour, the former working class of the rich world help their betters propel those same engines through their appetites and desires. No wonder the antagonism they once exhibited towards the wealthy has been mitigated; they are united with them to fuel the demand for continuous growth and expansion, seeing their best hope in the ever-increasing puchasing power that threatens to eat up the earth and everything on it. In order to make safe a ruinous system, they have been incorporated into it, thereby legitimizing its unsustainable and cannibalistic progress through the world.

It is no accident that at the very moment when the danger of irreparable damage to the planet becomes clear, the political and economic institutions of the West should be celebrating the universal acknowledgement of the superiority of the market system that is at the root of that damage. The need for a more stringent analysis and clarity of vision has been attended by a diminution and restriction of political debate, so that this becomes nothing more than a genteel disputation between liberals and conservatives who, whatever genuflexions they make to 'green issues', will do nothing to interfere with the dynamic of an industrialism whose voracious imperatives demand that the people devour the very earth that sustains them. That social democracy should have so little to say in face of such a development is perhaps the most bitter of the many silences that have descended where debate and argument should now be more passionately engaged than ever. The people who once looked to social democracy for such modest improvements, sufficiency and security, have seen that demand transformed into an imitation and caricature of the limitless predations of the rich. The quasi-universal exaltation of destructive forms of wealth that mysteriously impoverish even as they accumulate, makes a mockery of those fervent but frugal ambitions of a people who had never known anything but a gnawing want and ragged insufficiency.

An elaborate apparatus is required to prolong the illusion that the 'real world', in which we are constantly being exhorted to live, really is represented by that artificial construct defined by capitalism. This may convince the people of the rich world that traditional methods of accounting profit and loss are some kind of ultimate reality; but no such buttressing structures can any longer conceal from the poorest on earth that the degradation of the natural environment is a more compelling bottom line than anything conceived in either the musty counting-houses or the hi-tech citadels of capitalism.

For a time, the poor might have hoped that patterns of development initiated in the West could one day deliver them from their poverty. They were not to know either the inner desolation created by that version of wealth, or that the method of its production was never designed for their emancipation, but were, rather, calculated to lead them into dependency; a dependency which is similar to that set up in individuals attached to the life-support system of money which rules the lives of the rich.

At the very time when some people in the West are at last realizing that the market system, always growing and expanding, is unsustainable, real living alternatives in the world, ways of living that could offer a model of instruction and hope, are in their death-throes, on their way to extinction, ousted and superseded by the thrust of those same market forces.

15 ⁄ BYPASSING SUSTAINABLE SOCIETIES

The Chukchi and Nenets

THE PROCESS OF EXTINGUISHING even the vestiges of alternatives has not been confined to the capitalist model of industrialism. The pseudonymous Boris Komarov, whose *The Destruction of Nature in the Soviet Union** was published a decade ago by Pluto Press, long before *glasnost*, chronicled both the disregard by Soviet industry—with its desperate desire to compete with the West—of the consequences for the soil, air and waters of the country, and also the indifference to the values and practices of its own indigenous peoples, who were swept aside in the need for expansion. In particular, the alien implant of industrial society in the far north, and the settlers who took it there, were quite heedless of the effects, both on the terrain itself and on the people who had always lived there.

In 1917, the Soviet government obtained Siberia (a country in reserve), and the Far North in almost the same condition in which they were created by God, with the exception of the fur-bearing animals and gold. Hence the experiment in exploiting Siberia was a pure experiment, a kind of test for the socialist mode of development.

All northern communities are examples of organisms' equilibrium, at the brink of survival. Almost any disturbance by man destroys the fragile balance. Such gross disruptions as cutting trees in sparse forests and in the forest tundra have been catastrophic for

* Boris Komarov, *The Destruction of Nature in the Soviet Union*, (Pluto Press, 1979)

the land . . . Ten times more fuel per capita is burned in modern housing in Siberia than was burned in the tents and tepees of the natives. This has gravely affected the air in the settlements. Ten months of smoky atmosphere, filthy snow and dirty melt water kill all the moss in the surrounding area, and the bilberry ceases to bear fruit. Deprived of its covering of moss and lichen, the permafrost quickly turns into a swamp. In the opinion of specialists, production of automobile and tractor motors adapted to the severe northern weather would help more than anything to ease the smog. There is nothing strange in this; since it is impossible to start their motors in the mornings, the drivers frequently let the vehicles run all night in neutral, and of course, air pollution increases.

The settlers in the North have gone there as colonists:

The modern era of development in Siberia and the North has not made the settlers into a group of people vitally interested in sensible nonpredatory use of the new lands. Development today is urban industrial colonization, a foreign body both for nature and the native peoples of Siberia and the North.

For the 'white man' arriving with the best of intentions, the North is a white desert, regardless of what grows there and what does not; it is a void that must be filled with the meaning and light of the European industrial way of life. In sum, it gets filled with garbage. But it all begins with psychology; here is how a journalist quite convinced of the correctness and virtue of 'progress' describes the tundra: 'I looked across the map illuminator. Below us was the unpeopled and lifeless tundra. Across the barren earth, dotted with swamps, was sparse, frail and fragile lichen—and emptiness; neither beast nor bird nor even smoke on the horizon. A sense of dead silence and tangible primitiveness. As if we were no longer on the earth but on another lifeless planet that had not yet been touched by the breath of life.'

For a Chukchi or Nenets (the native peoples of the north) the 'dead lifeless tundra' is just as vital a world as France or Greece is for a European or the Sahara for a Bedouin. The local deer herder sees thousands of nuances of life inaccessible to the newcomer. He finds his flocks from their reflection on low-lying clouds dozens of kilometres away; the language of the northern people has not just one word for 'snow'—there are dozens of words for every possible kind of snow: blizzard, drift, falling, dry, moist.

Until recently the world of the tundra was for its people a special world, with spirits reincarnated in rocks, in the underground warm tundra, with its myths, embodying truths of human existence no less profound than the mythologies of other peoples.

The children raised from the first grade onward in boarding schools retain few of the cultural attributes of their nation. The children know both Russian and their own language poorly; they forget the work habits of their fathers and grandfathers, while they absorb all the worst aspects of modern urban civilization . . . Many of the Northerners can no longer even be ascribed any nationality as far as way of life and physical and psychological characteristics are concerned—unless it is the 'Russian alcoholic civilization', since drunkenness begins here at the age of thirteen or fourteen.

In the past their way of life was intimately bound up with the course of natural phenomena and totally depended on variations in the climate and animal population. Even if total ecological balance between environment and man here was doubtful, the economy was stable. During cold periods, the number of deer increased sharply, and the tribes migrated into the tundra. Ten to fifteen years later it warmed up, epizootics decimated the deer, and the tribes returned to the seashore to hunt for marine animals. They preserved their tools and the habits of flexible adaptation to local conditions; shifting from nomadic to a settled life and back again.

Today's methods of deer-raising and fishing on collective farms and state farms, the entire planned economy, simply pay no attention to the dynamics of natural conditions, to cool snaps, heat waves . . . The dynamics of the plan are always the same, whether in the black belt or the north; year in, year out, constant growth in output.

Modern science cannot cope with its main task in society: to ensure the survival of this society. Soviet ecology cannot even cope with part of this task. It does not even have the courage to warn us about the impending danger.

Komarov estimates that of the twenty-two million square kilometres of the Soviet Union, one third is uninhabitable—water, perpetual ice and snow, barren rock. That leaves around fourteen million square kilometres. Of this, five hundred thousand square kilometres are barren lands and swamps left by deforestation, logging and fires; two hundred thousand square kilometres mutilated by mining and peat works; fifty thousand square kilometres covered by dumps, slag, sludge heaps, municipal dumps or mines; one hundred and twenty thousand square kilometres are buried under waters of reservoirs; six hundred and thirty thousand square kilometres of eroded land, ravines and dunes where fields were. He assesses the extent of sterile waste at 1.45 million square kilometres—that is ten per cent of the inhabitable territory—equal to the size of Western Europe, which is 1.4 million square kilometres.

Beneath the hesitant pulsations of conciliation and hostility between the Soviet Union and the United States, beneath the moralistic terms in which the merits of 'capitalism' and 'communism' are argued, another, more material struggle is taking place. If the United States hopes to bankrupt the Soviet Union in an intensifying competition for supremacy in arms (an achievement which the triumphalism of Bush suggests has already been reached), the resources and land mass of the Soviet Union are potentially far greater than those of the United States and can be used to strategic advantage: for all the poisonings and contaminations, the Soviet Union still possesses physical frontiers within its own border that have yet to be 'conquered'. That the whole world may lose as a result of this malign and, for the most part, subterranean rivalry, cannot, of course, be expected to disturb those who are conducting such sublime ideological struggles in the interests of such resounding abstractions as History or Free Markets.

Unhappily, even the most helpful scenario that optimists of both East and West have sketched for the future—the convergence of interests between the United States and the Soviet Union, the reintegration of the Soviet economy into the rest of the world—offers little comfort to the world's poor. If there is a *rapprochement* between the two world-systems, this is likely to be a coming together of the rich and the relatively rich, and their realization that they have a common antagonist; any budding amity between them is likely to be cemented by the threat to them of hundreds of millions of hungry and excluded people. This amounts to a collusion of the privileged, who see a dawning common purpose in keeping for themselves the dwindling resources which might have lifted the rest of humanity out of poverty and wretchedness.

Such convergence already exists. The rich of the West and the élite of the Soviet Union display a common attitude towards the consequences of their competitive generosity with the pollutants and contaminants which they have poured upon the earth. The zealots of the market economy believe that the rich will be able to buy themselves a safe passage out of the poisoned earth. Market forces—those despoilers of the planet—are themselves going to buy exemption for those with the deepest purses from the consequences of their own actions. Mrs Thatcher declared after the Paris 'summit' of July 1989 that only the creation of more wealth will pay to clear up the damage caused by the creation of wealth in the first place. In the Soviet Union, says Komarov:

> The avant-garde of the people, as some of the representatives of the ruling élite call themselves, perceives the acuity of ecological problems only from the figures in various documents. The green fences around their suburban houses effectively screen them from the effects of both the economic and the ecological crises. Five to six per cent of our society has access to natural products, special drinking water and special swimming pools with filtered sea-water (without oil and phenol).

The Warlis

In a very different climatic zone from that of the people of the tundra, the *adivasis* or tribals of India, are resisting the eclipse and disgracing of their sustainable way of life, and are seeking to rescue traditions that are being smothered by forms of 'development' that have their origin in distant foreign cultures. This concern with sustainability has nothing to do with nostalgia; the living practice of another relationship with the natural world is the hope and pledge of our survival. If it has to do with the past, it is even more urgently linked to all our futures.

The interest of the Greens in Europe in sustainability is viewed with detachment by many people in India. After all, the ancient Hindus had worked out the principle of *Sanata Dharma*—the harmony pervading the whole universe; and from this was derived the *Svadharma*, the personal moral conduct of the individual. (Such concepts are not, of course, confined to Hinduism, but are to be found in practically all religions.)

All living creatures were seen to be dependent on each other and on the non-living universe too. This mutual dependence is contained in the saying *Jeevo Jeevasya Jeevanan*: 'A living creature derives life from another living creature'. The *Mahabharata* recommends that people should follow a 'mode of living which is founded upon a total harmlessness towards all creatures, or (in the case of absolute necessity) upon a minimum of such harm'. From this we arrive at a code of conduct based on respect for all life, a belief that all creatures, including human beings, should be treated as of equal intrinsic worth and value. It is this that should distinguish our morality from the generally prevailing one which recognizes only 'human rights', and does not even implement these.

On the non-living side, we have the concept of the *Panch Mahabhutas*, the five basic elements: *prithvi* (earth), *aap* (water), *tejas* (fire or light), *vayu* (air), *akasa* (space). *Bhutas* are living beings; *mahabhutas* are prior to living beings, since the very existence and survival of the latter are dependent upon the former. Therefore, the *Mahabhutas* occupy a revered place in Indian philosophy. 'All living beings are born and evolve out of the five *Mahabhutas*, and in death they go back to them.'

This is of such central importance that it needs to be elaborated. A stone that exists today is worn out by erosion, its constituents forming soil, from which elements are taken up by plants which are then eaten by animals. The stone today could be part of us tomorrow. And when we die, the elements go back into the soil to be cycled and recycled indefinitely. Water and air are recycled even faster while we are still alive, and spread wider. The water that makes up eighty-five per cent of our bodies can reach the other side of the earth, and be incorporated into the body of someone else; in that sense, we are, literally, part of one another. The oxygen which we breathe provides us with energy, and together with part of our food, becomes carbon dioxide which, exhaled, can again be picked up by plants anywhere on earth. All of us occupy space today which was occupied by something else in the past, and will be in the future. We are all one with the universe.

It isn't just that 'no man is an island', but that every man and woman is, or may become, a part of everything in the world. The inanimate elements today are incarnated, made flesh tomorrow, and what is incarnate in one living thing becomes reincarnated in a number of others through time. Perhaps this is the meaning of reincarnation: it is the basis on which so many of the earth's resources become 'renewable'.

After the principles of 'least harm' or 'least interference' and the *Mahabhutas*, the third ancient Indian principle is that of the cyclical nature of things, all things, from the smallest creature to the universe. A sustainable system, that is, one that can go on indefinitely in time, can be either in total equilibrium or cyclical. Total equilibrium means that there is no change at all. But all living creatures change—they are born, they grow, they die; so total equilibrium means total death. A cyclical system, however, allows for change, provided that there is no 'waste' produced. And this is where natural systems are perfect; there is no garbage of any kind whatsoever in nature. It is only humans, with their ability and will to dominate nature, who can, and do, produce waste.

What is so remarkable about these principles is that they evolved when there was no threat to survival from disappearing natural resources or environmental pollution. The ability of our ancestors to foresee that these were necessary for human existence at that time indicates the brilliance of their thought. For it is only in the last two decades that Western ecologists and environmentalists claim to have 'discovered' some of these basic truths.

Just what violence industrialism does to the *mahabhutas*, by taking the conquest of nature as the basic datum for development, can be seen more clearly in India, where sustainable civilization has been built on the principles of respect for nature, the use of its products and creatures in a manner to satisfy basic needs that does not jeopardize their continued life and growth. In any case, the conquest of nature is a deeply contradictory idea; as human beings are also part of the natural world, who is conquering whom? Doubly ironic is the fact that the enthusiasts of economic growth and development argue that greed is human nature, which is both ineradicable and unconquerable. They see the domination of all aspects of nature, except that which they attribute to human beings, as essential for their purposes. By encouraging the unfettered indulgence of an indomitable human nature (appetites), they set in motion a dynamic process that is calculated to eat up the natural resources that have been subdued by the legitimate and unstoppable voracity of human beings. In this way, the engines of the Western economic system are not merely external machines which work their harm over the crust of the planet (the environment); human need has been yoked to them. The rich of the earth—that means a majority in the West, together with the élites of the countries of the South—have internalized economic necessity in such a way that they can no longer distinguish this from the needs of human beings. This is why the surviving examples of alternatives are so precious, and at such risk of being ground into extinction.

The Warli tribal people of Northern Maharashtra in Western India have for millennia lived in symbiotic balance with their forest environment. In February 1988, near Dahanu, a thousand Warli people protested, following the inspiration of the *Chipko* movement, against the selling of forest land by the State government to private contractors. They protected the threatened trees with their own bodies to prevent felling. Their cry was *jangal bachao, manao bachao*—'save the forests, save the people', for their identification with the forest is complete. Deforestation has degraded the living conditions of many thousands of tribal people in this, as in so many other areas, not only of India, but the whole world. To make matters worse, those who have always lived in harmony with the forests are being accused of damaging them. Ever since the British introduced their infamous Forestry Acts in the mid-nineteenth century, the *adivasis* have been criminalized, stigmatized as 'encroachers', and blamed for the spoliation of the environment that has nurtured them, and which they have nurtured, for at least four thousand years.

The removal of the rich, organic diversity of their natural forest, and its replacement by monocultures of teak or subabul trees, has profoundly wounded the lives of the tribal people, and undermined a culture whose richness is a direct reflection of the multitudinous life-forms that exist in the natural forest.

Animist, their aetiological myth places at the beginning of time a couple who had created themselves, Mahadev and Ganga-Gauri. These two produced life on earth by sowing seeds which grew so luxuriantly that the cattle multiplied until they were so densely packed that their horns touched each other. However, the burden on Dhartari, the earth, was too much to bear, so she sought help from Pandudev; but instead of helping her, he repulsed and insulted her. Mahadev, Dhartari's elder brother, was angered by this rejection of his sister, and when he distributed the kingdoms, he gave Pandu the Kingdom of Death. Pandu tried to flee Death, but was pursued relentlessly until Death claimed him.

In this story, Death came to earth because Mother Earth had been insulted; a prescient warning, perhaps, to those who believe the earth to be a limitless absorber of their toxins, whether material or spiritual. After Dhartari, the most revered goddesses of the Warlis are Kansari, Corn Goddess and Gavtari, Cow Goddess. Land and cattle to plough it are essential to produce the grain for their survival, and they are all treated as sacred.

Although nature in the form of tropical forests is bountiful, the Warlis use its products sparingly. They extract just enough for their own sustenance, apparently being aware that over-exploitation can result only in their own destruction. Their homes are simple structures of mud, sticks and thatch, using renewable materials only, and are appropriate to the climate. Their cattle are housed with them, and the huts are always resplendently clean.

An important tradition of the Warlis is the painting on the mud walls of the goddess Palghat. The painting, known as the *chowk*, is done with rice flour, and plays an important part in the marriage ceremony. Palghat is a fertility symbol, and is depicted with her consort Panchshiriya, and is surrounded with an ornamental frame. It is from this tradition that Warli art has developed.

The paintings are on a background of mud on cloth or paper. They show the daily occupations and activities, the environment with its abundance of life. From ploughing and sowing to harvesting and threshing; hunting and fishing, collecting firewood and cooking, drawing water from the well; musical instruments, especially the *tarpa*—made from a dried gourd, baskets, pottery and the implements of their labour; a variety of trees, often stylized, and especially animals: tigers, monkeys, monitor lizards, cattle, poultry, peacocks and many other forest birds, right down to the smallest creatures—the rats, ants and spiders. Above all, there are the representations of the gods and goddesses, the dances that mark their feasts and their joyful celebration of life itself. The forest is where the *hira dev* (green god) lives, where the sweet resins and secretions of the wood give nourishment and meaning.

The paintings of the Warlis are much admired, and hang on the walls of the well-to-do in Bombay, Hamburg and London. At the same time as their art is marketed, their annihilation draws closer, for the same market system that sells their work to sophisticated metropolitan connoisseurs in the West also requires their trees for industrial and urban development. Most of the trees are cut down to make furniture and building products, for pulp and rayon. Still more is exported to earn foreign exchange with which luxuries for the élite can be imported.

The destruction of the *adivasi* environment is only a fraction of that breaking of forest cultures and traditions that the market economy has inflicted world-wide. There are about nine million different wildlife species in the world, many of which could be used to benefit humanity, if they were not being destroyed before their full value is assessed. Today, a mere twenty plant species produce ninety per cent of the world's food. But more than one hundred and fifty species have been cultivated on a large scale in the not remote past; and eighty thousand species are believed to be edible. *Adivasis* have a tremendous store of knowledge of what wild plants can be eaten, when they can be eaten, and how they must be cooked.

A few decades ago, there were fifty thousand varieties of paddy being planted in India. If present trends continue, by the end of the century there will be less than fifty varieties in use. This trend is dangerous, because each variety can survive under different climatic conditions and is resistant to different kinds of pest. By relying on only a few strains, we expose ourselves to a terrible danger; a single new pest can destroy a large amount of our paddy production, when only a few high-yielding varieties are planted. The lesson ought to have been assimilated from the consequences of the Irish potato famine. Not a single strain from the Andes could resist the universal blight that struck in the 1840s. *Adivasis* have always planted many traditional kinds of paddy, so they never become reliant on a single strain.

The destruction of the forests also leads to the extinction of alternative forms of fertilizer and pesticide; chemicalized agriculture leaves poisons that remain in soil and water for many years. These poisons are taken up by plants and the animals that eat them, and at every stage they become more concentrated and cause more and more damage. Plants such as kadu limb (*azadiactha indica*), adulsa (*adhatoda vasica*), vekhand (*acorus calamus*) and many others can provide safe pesticides to protect crops and stored food; they can be obtained free, or at low cost, wherever these plants grow; but with the eviction of the *adivasis* from their ancestral lands, the knowledge of these things is extinguished together with the plants themselves.

Most of the requirements of fertilizer can also be obtained from plants, and proper use of them can increase food production considerably. Plants such as dhedar (*sesbania spp*), takla (*cassia tora*), kuhili (*mucuna pruriens*) that grow wild can contribute to enhanced yield of crops.

Over thirty per cent of Western medicines are made from plants, and in India, many more. Sales of medicines from plants and animals in the United States are more than a billion dollars a year. For instance, the common Konkan plant, harkaya or sarpagandha (*rauvolfia serpentina*) has been used in India for four thousand years to treat snakebites, nervous disorders, dysentery, cholera and fever. It was only about forty years ago that Western medicine 'discovered' it, and it became one of the most important drugs for treating some kinds of mental illness and heart disease in the West. Because of this one plant, millions of people in the West are enabled to lead normal lives. But because it is so much in demand, this plant has practically disappeared from the forests of India.

Some species of yams (*dioscores spp*), piva (*costus speciosus*) and even methi (*trigonella foenum-graecum*) contain a chemical called diosgenin, which is used for the preparation of oral contraceptives and drugs against arthritis, rheumatic fever, sciatica and several skin diseases. Another common plant, sadaphuli (*caranthus roseus*) has over seventy-five chemicals in its leaves and roots. Two very important drugs which can cure some kinds of previously incurable cancer are taken from it.

In the living practice of *adivasi* society, use of traditional herbal medicines which are available at little cost, is still widespread. Many of the big drug manufacturing transnationals have set up expensive laboratories in India, to develop medicines from plants, which they will then sell back to local people at high prices. The depletion of traditional knowledge thus feeds the growth and expansion of a vast value-added allopathic medicine system.

With the destruction of over one million hectares of forest every year in India alone, it is not simply 'timber' that is being used up. Indeed, timber is the inert commodity defined by economists, with all the vital life-giving associations crushed out of it. It is a question of the degradation of an irreplaceable way of living from which we have everything to learn.

In the substitution of the monoculture of a single species for the diverse, sheltering habitat of the Warlis, we can see a metaphor for a world-wide process. For the richness and variety of all traditional cultures are being extinguished in the monoculture of money, a mutation in which human beings become the most lucrative cash-crop of all. People are the highest-yielding variety ever conceived, and even though they require certain expensive inputs, they bear much of their own cost, and they reproduce themselves; and so much of the crop can be exploited! So many qualities, abilities, attributes that can be converted into commodities and sold back to them; the potential for bringing to market, for harvesting, for monetizing is unlimited. People are grown for profit like any other natural resource, the most raw material of all, infinitely pliable and adaptable, not only in its labour, but in its deepest needs and desires. The real crime of the Warlis is that they have resisted full entry into the market economy, and retain enough of an alternative to threaten the totalizing monoculture of the markets.

In India, the ancient sages retired to the forest in search of wisdom. Their understanding was that without a respect for all things, both living and inanimate, human beings cannot develop fully. The unquiet life of the late-twentieth century makes it more important than ever that the retreat into the forest remains possible. Yet what wisdom would we find in the barren plantations of monoculture, other than a reflection of our own inner desolation?*

* Jeremy Seabrook, *The Race for Riches*, (Green Print 1988), contains further material on the Warlis. Also, Winin Pereira's *Forestry, Farming and Survival in India*, (Earthscan, to be published 1990), considers in greater depth the situation of tribal peoples in Northern Maharashtra.

16 / CAPITALISM AND THE INNER LIFE

T HOSE WHO OPPOSE THE BRUTAL NECESSITIES of capitalism
have always had to tread carefully in any discussion of the life of the
spirit; an over-reaction against the abuse of religion as a social discipline
in the early capitalist era has inhibited attempts at an elaboration of what
the life of the spirit might mean in an alternative society. This has, in
particular, been profoundly disabling to the socialist endeavour, for,
naturally enough, capitalist society has not neglected the spaces obligingly
left vacant by its antagonists; on the contrary, this has been the site of its
most careful attention and deepest penetration.

The dismissal by many socialists of the realm of the spirit, doubtless
under the promptings of a consciousness defined, however distantly, by
Marx, means that there is a vast territory open to reclamation by the
Greens.

For all human societies, in one way or another, acknowledge the importance of the spiritual life, accommodate people's need for times of reflection and contemplation, recognize our efforts to reconcile a longing for
permanency with the fact of our mortality, and provide ways in which the
individual might reach wisdom, in her or his own way. In their traditional
forms, however, these activities are far too immaterial and self-reliant to
be left untouched by an avid and restless market-system, whose deepest
purpose is to make profit, out of the most basic human needs and out of
the most secret areas of experience alike. Accordingly, a substitute must
be found for the inner life; an exalted function which, in our time, has
devolved upon the power of *fantasy*. For this is the closest approximation
that capitalist entrepreneurs can devise to religion. Fantasy is perhaps best
defined as imaginings and yearnings that can be facilitated through

material symbols, and that may serve to compensate in some measure for the scarrings and blightings of the inner landscape. 'I feel empty inside' is a common enough lament; in our society this bears a dynamic relation to the abundance without. Such inner desolation can be remedied only by a series of increasingly ingenious purchases—sensations, experiences, commodities, that will occupy, however briefly and unsatisfactorily, the ruined and trampled spaces within.

Thus, even those areas of human concern least amenable to it can be made to turn in a handsome profit. The decay of religion in the West is far more advanced than anything that has been achieved in the avowedly atheistic Communist States which have actively sought to suppress religious belief. This is perhaps yet another measure of the adaptability and subtlety of capitalist society in comparison with the lumbering machinery of a socialism which cannot even compete in the one area in which it has always laid claim to undisputed supremacy— that of ideology.

Of course, many of the ministrations formerly in the hands of the servants of the churches have already been taken from them and dispersed in a complex division of labour elsewhere. Some of these have become the preserve of those secular purveyors of consolation, comfort and counsel, those professions whose high calling involves them in the leading of other people's lives; others have been appropriated by those who make a substantial living out of encouraging individuals to find personal solutions to socially produced miseries. And even what remains—that which might have been considered inalienable, has nevertheless been transformed by extensive and high-yielding investment in fantasy.

The saving of souls in the wealthy, materialistic societies of the West seems, at first sight, a vain and archaic undertaking. A version of salvation, however, remains. This is to be seen, not as having anything to do with the immortality or ultimate destiny of the soul; nor does it mean the attainment of wisdom. It is not a search for truth and meaning; not even a coming to terms with the self and its limitations. If it is seen as a seeking after happiness, this should not be confused with that feeling associated with religious exaltation, enlightenment or peace, but is rather a form of absolute satisfaction in the here and now, a kind of transcendent satiation of the senses, a sort of conquest of time; in other words, something formerly assumed—perhaps correctly—to be simply not available in this life.

The feelings of aloneness, inadequacy and incompleteness which all individuals in some degree experience, are no longer the object of the consolations of religion; but have been annexed by an economic and social order which promises that remedies do exist, even for sufferings that are clearly unavoidable, existential. This miracle can be accomplished only through the sacrament of money, a secular form of divine grace.

This is how the market-system succeeds, not only in being sanctified, but also in appearing to offer a way of transcendence. Fantasy—the vending of images, shadows, semblances of perfection and wholeness—is the commodity which corresponds to this usurped religious activity; not the flesh and blood, not the living presence of the fabulous icons of the culture, the heroes and stars and celebrities, but their likeness, or appearance, their *image* must answer our thirst for revelation, for reconciliation with our own inadequacies. We don't need to come to terms with our own shortcomings; we can transcend them with the help of these projected phantasms and compensatory images. Fantasy is a promise of perfection materialized; small wonder that there is such a brisk market in it. The models paraded before the people overflow with beauty, goodness, prowess, strength, all conceivable talents and attainments. Even the rooms of smallest children (and this is, perhaps, why it is considered essential that every child has a right to privacy) are hung with figures of fantasy, untainted with contact with living flesh; models that propose the unreachable, but give corporeal shape to desires and longings that might once have been considered inexpressible. The effect is to set up further dissatisfactions, to which an apparent response will be offered in due course by the system to which all children are apprenticed as trainee consumers from earliest infancy.

Most religious teachings involve the acceptance in this life of limitations and disappointments; some urge us to make the best of the qualities we do possess, while we become reconciled to an absence of those attributes we might have desired. Capitalist fantasy offers an advance on such modest ambition. Indeed, the lucrative commerce in shadows, particularly those which serve sexual imaginings, merely excite further morbid desire for the unattainable. Whole industries are devoted to persuading us that we need never confront our limitations; indeed, the buoyancy of such enterprises depends absolutely upon our not reaching wisdom or maturity, but, on the contrary, upon the prolonging of hankerings and the arousal of discontents which we might, perhaps, in another context, have learned to come to terms with. Rather than promoting human growth, these processes actually stunt and inhibit it. A state of chronic and aggravated longing is obviously ripe for development by those who can offer the transfigurings of fantasy. There is something awesome, that commands the reluctant admiration even of those appalled by a system that has the self-confidence to trade in this way in human failings and frailties, and which can make substantial fortunes for those who do not demur at such exotic forms of private, even secretive, enterprise. That the roots of violence in rich Western societies might also be sought in this dangerous and destructive commerce cannot be expected to be of concern to those for whom the highest endeavour is the making of a killing; but they should not be astonished if, as a result, the society they uphold so strenuously is as a consequence, penetrated by a smell of death.

The most powerful agents of social control in our time are not the coercive agents of the State, strong and extensive as these are; not the army or police; nor are they the wholesome disciplines of money, preached by conservatives; and certainly not the educators and instructors whose ostensible business is with teaching the young right from wrong. The greatest controlling force, the most rigorous and unflinching mechanism whereby social order is maintained, what makes these divided and strife-prone and unfair societies cohere is the overwhelming, pervasive, sweet and delusive power of fantasy, which is a kind of ideological emanation of the market economy.

It should not surprise us that this is so, nor how it comes to be. The widely commented decay of manufacturing industry in the rich West, and the suppression of much necessary labour, particularly that which was connected with the making of things that are demonstrably useful, leaves a vacuum waiting to be filled. The extinction in Britain of the making of many material necessities takes away those functions which lent the people so strong a sense of place and purpose. The empty psychological spaces in the lives of people—which correspond to the deserted sites of mines, mills and factories—are increasingly occupied by a wild luxuriance of fantasy, just as invasive weeds and willow-herb overrun the abandoned locations, the ruined places where things were once made.

If religion was exploited by capital as a means of disciplining a refractory labour force in the early industrial period, it is only to be expected that the life of the spirit should once more be a controlling mechanism that maintains the subordination of the people in capitalism's version of leisure; although, naturally, a life of privation, scarcity and hunger required a different mode of spiritual rigour from that in which the marketing of its plethoric superfluities is a primary objective. Nor should we imagine that any 'post-industrial society' liberates us from the influence of capitalist labour: the lives of the people, in even the richest societies, remain dominated by and dependent upon it, even though many who now perform that labour may no longer be visible, spirited away, as they have been, into the slums, shanties and barracks of South Korea, Brazil or South Africa. It is partly to conceal this relationship that the mills of fantasy work night and day in the rich world, weaving strange new fabrics; new wants and desires are struck in the white heat of its forges; the deepest longings are mined in its bottomless pits; powerful dissatisfactions are quarried in its unending search for profit.

The fantasy of happiness in this life is the pie come down from the sky; it proves to be no more edible than it was when its consumption was postponed indefinitely. But it did succeed, for a moment, in displacing alternatives. It is the absence of these which leaves such ample space for the hopes and visions of the Greens to be realized.

17 ⁄ CONCLUSION

To critics of the markets, its defenders will sooner or later say 'Well what would you put in its place?' This conundrum should more properly be thrown back at the advocates of the system themselves; what are they proposing to put in place of the exhausted earth, the depleted resources, the contaminated water and vitiated air? If it had been the purpose of humanity on earth to bring to the edge of ruin the planet itself, no more efficient mechanism could have been invented than the market system itself, with its prodigious use of energy and materials in the sublime mission of replacing as much of human activity with commodities and the monetary transactions that attend them. The market should play a minimal and functional role in our lives; and to those who ask what should we then do, the answer is: expel the market from all those spaces it has inappropriately invaded, reclaim autonomy and self-reliance wherever this is possible. The market cannot create social justice, it is powerless to distinguish between good and evil; it has no moral role, even less should it be the object of the curious cults that have grown around its mythic power in the West.

Everywhere in the world, alternatives have been suppressed, and continue to be destroyed at an accelerating pace in the face of its invasive power, the most deadly of all colonizations, because it insinuates itself into the spirit and the imagination of people. In its presence, older patterns of self-reliance and non-monetized ways of answering human need are being eliminated. The inferiorizing of traditional customs and patterns of living, the images of 'backwardness', the curse of 'underdevelopment' are part of the same global spectacle—the subordination of the most shining examples of self-reliance to the spread of the Western system.

CONCLUSION

Whatever the benefits of a single global-market, the survival of alternatives will not be one of them. This suggests a level of total control to dwarf all previous tyrannies and totalitarianisms; the dictatorship of the market.

If alternatives are to be rediscovered, retained or reformulated, they will require the same energy and passion deployed by those who are moved by the profound conviction that all future development must be determined by an extension of what exists already. Until now, resistance to these processes has been diffuse and often ill co-ordinated. It needs now to be concentrated and drawn together, so that it matches the vigour and intensity of those who would lock the whole planet into submission to forms of development that will make our freedom to choose otherwise nothing more than melancholy dreams and extinguished yearnings for what might have been.